Many blessings!
May this be a day
of great favor and
joy.
We celebrate your life
today.

Rachel Hickson

Run Your Race

Run Your Race

SOMETHING TO LIVE FOR... SOMETHING WORTH DYING FOR!

A 40 DAY INSPIRATIONAL

TO FOCUS YOUR LIFE

WITH PURPOSE AND PASSION

RACHEL HICKSON

MONARCH
BOOKS
Oxford, UK & Grand Rapids, Michigan, USA

First published in the UK in 2012 by Monarch Books
(a publishing imprint of Lion Hudson plc)
Wilkinson House, Jordan Hill Road, Oxford OX2 8DR, England
Tel: +44 (0)1865 302750 Fax: +44 (0)1865 302757
Email: monarch@lionhudson.com
www.lionhudson.com

ISBN 978 0 85721 031 9

Distributed by:
UK: Marston Book Services, PO Box 269, Abingdon, Oxon, OX14 4YN
USA: Kregel Publications, PO Box 2607, Grand Rapids, Michigan 49501

British Library Cataloguing Data
A catalogue record for this book is available from the British Library.

Printed and bound in China.

I dedicate this book to the
courageous generations in the
Middle East who are determined
to run their race and finish like
their Champion, Jesus.

CONTENTS

ACKNOWLEDGMENTS

This is the hardest part of the book to write as there are so many who have helped this project become a reality. As always, I want to thank my precious husband who gives me space to write. He is my greatest cheerleader!

I also want to thank Tony Collins and the Lion Hudson team for their professional support and attention to detail as we have discussed the publication of this book. It has been a joy to work with you – thank you!

I also owe a debt of thanks to Helen Azer. She has proofread the text, examined my spelling, researched the quotes and stories, corrected my grammar and helped me sound intelligent. Thank you for all your reading time!

Thank you David, my son, for your time considering the layout, design and imagery of this book. You have an amazing eye for style and I have loved your input too.

Finally thank **you** for buying this book.

I hope it will be a catalyst that will rekindle your dreams and stir up a fresh hunger for God and His word, so that you can enjoy your life with a greater sense of passion and purpose.

INTRODUCTION

BEWARE – this is a dangerous book.

> **2 Timothy 4:7**
> I have fought the good fight, I have finished the race, I have kept the faith.

This book has the power to change your life! This inspiring collection has been written with the desire to help you focus your life so that you run passionately after God. I want these readings to trigger your resolve to give your life away completely and fulfil every purpose of God for which you were made. It is time to run your race of destiny vigorously, ready to die if necessary, but more determined to live life on the cutting edge. God wants a tribe of dangerous people who will give their life away and see His kingdom come. We need to be ready, armed, and dangerous, with the word of God burning in our hearts. We need to pay the price of obedient sacrifice, learn from the heroes of faith who have walked before us, and stand with courage and conviction. God wants us to be part of a new movement of radical lovers who will run without fear, abandoned to the will of God.

Many of us start life with a burning zeal that believes we can change the world with Jesus, but then fears and excuses distract us, causing us to lose our focus and doubt our ability to run this race of life. If you sometimes feel like this, I have written this set of devotions for you. Allow God to breathe His life into your being and reawaken your sense of destiny and purpose. Let your dreams and passions be expressed, do not hide them any longer. Listen to the shout of heaven and the heroes who have lived before us, and take your place in history. Decide that this is the time for **you** to run your race!

Therefore, since we are surrounded by such a great cloud of witnesses, let us throw off everything that hinders and the sin that so easily entangles, and let us run with perseverance the race marked out for us. Let us fix our eyes on Jesus, the author and perfecter of our faith, who for the joy set before him endured the cross, scorning its shame, and sat down at the right hand of the throne of God.

Hebrews 12:1–2

Experts tell us that it takes three weeks of concerted effort to break a negative pattern of behaviour and a total of six weeks to establish a new pattern and lifestyle. So, this will be forty days (six weeks) of "medicine" from the word of God specifically designed to help you re-establish your priorities to be in alignment with the call of God on your life. Decide today to read a dangerous book and let the word of God activate your passion for Jesus again.

So let us pray:

Father, I want to dedicate these forty days to You. I desire to serve You without fear. I want to give my life away for kingdom purpose,

to touch nations, and to minister to people.

I know that as I take this focused time to talk to You about the passions of my heart You will meet with me. So, stir my heart to love You more deeply and serve You more completely. Fill me with a fresh sense of purpose and courage. Reveal Your plans for my life. Let me walk with You in a new level of intimacy and obedience.

Thank You for my race of destiny. Let me focus my eyes on the race before me and complete this race like a champion. Father, I thank You that You made me to run and finish excellently!

Activate me, reignite me, accelerate me into every purpose. Amen.

So what is the next step? These meditations have been written as a forty-day series, with a fresh challenge each week. Each of these challenges will focus on an aspect of your character and will train you to be a better champion in this race of life.

The six challenges are as follows:

Week 1 – Dedicated Heroes
Week 2 – Determined Courage
Week 3 – Devoted to Purity
Week 4 – Disciplined Sacrifice
Week 5 – Dangerous Passion
Week 6 – Destined as Champions

Each day you will read a portion of Scripture, activate your purpose and then release your heart cry to God in prayer. You should try to find a place where you can be alone and focus as you do this. If possible, first deal with any situation that could interrupt you: turn your phone off and make this your time to concentrate on your mission! Later, towards the end of the week, find time to read all the devotions for the topic in one sitting and let the challenge of the week stir your spirit.

I believe that as you do this, you will watch the word of God begin to refocus your vision and ignite your passion. The word will reawaken your destiny, enable you to think clearly, and teach you to take back what the enemy has stolen through your fear or disobedience.

So let us run the race of our life and cross the finishing line like champions!

Rachel Hickson

GET UP AND WIN THE RACE

I

"Quit! Give up! You're beaten!"
They shout at me and plead,
"There's just too much against you
    now.
This time you can't succeed."

And as I start to hang my head
In front of failure's face,
My downward fall is broken by
The memory of a race.

And hope refills my weakened will
As I recall that scene;
For just the thought of that short
    race
rejuvenates my being.

II

A children's race – young boys,
    young men –
How I remember well.
Excitement, sure! But also fear;
It wasn't hard to tell.

They all lined up so full of hope.
Each thought to win that race.
Or tie for first, or if not that,
At least take second place.

And fathers watched from off the
    side
Each cheering for his son.
And each boy hoped to show his
    dad
That he would be the one.

The whistle blew and off they went
Young hearts and hopes of fire.
To win and be the hero there
Was each young boy's desire.

And one boy in particular
Whose dad was in the crowd
Was running near the lead and
    thought:
"My dad will be so proud!"

But as they speeded down the field
Across a shallow dip,

The little boy who thought to win
Lost his step and slipped.

Trying hard to catch himself
His hands flew out to brace,
And mid the laughter of the crowd
He fell flat on his face.

So down he fell and with him hope
– He couldn't win it now –
Embarrassed, sad, he only wished
To disappear somehow.

But as he fell his dad stood up
And showed his anxious face,
Which to the boy so clearly said,
"Get up and win the race!"

He quickly rose, no damage done
– Behind a bit, that's all –
And ran with all his mind and might
To make up for his fall.

So anxious to restore himself
– To catch up and to win –
His mind went faster than his legs:
He slipped and fell again!

He wished that he had quit before
With only one disgrace.
"I'm hopeless as a runner now;
I shouldn't try to race."

But in the laughing crowd he
searched
And found his father's face;
That steady look which said again:
"Get up and win the race."

So up he jumped to try again
– Ten yards behind the last –
"If I'm to gain those yards," he
thought,
"I've got to move real fast."

Exerting everything he had
He regained eight or ten,
But trying so hard to catch the lead
He slipped and fell again!

Defeat! He lay there silently
– A tear dropped from his eye –
"There's no sense running anymore;
Three strikes: I'm out! Why try!"

The will to rise had disappeared;
All hope had fled away;
So far behind, so error prone;
A loser all the way.

"I've lost, so what's the use," he
      thought
"I'll live with my disgrace."
But then he thought about his
      dad
Who soon he'd have to face.

"Get up," an echo sounded low.
"Get up and take your place;
You were not meant for failure
      here.
Get up and win the race."

"With borrowed will get up," it
      said,
"You haven't lost at all.
For winning is no more than this:
To rise each time you fall."

So up he rose to run once more,
And with a new commit
He resolved that win or lose
At least he wouldn't quit.

So far behind the others now
– The most he'd ever been –
Still he gave it all he had
And ran as though to win.

Three times he'd fallen,
      stumbling;
Three times he rose again;
Too far behind to hope to win
He still ran to the end.

They cheered the winning runner
As he crossed the line first place.
Head high, and proud, and
      happy;
no falling, no disgrace.

But when the fallen youngster
Crossed the line last place,
The crowd gave him the greater
      cheer,
For finishing the race.

And even though he came in last
With head bowed low, unproud,
You would have thought he'd
      won the race
To listen to the crowd.

And to his dad he sadly said,
"I didn't do too well."
"To me, you won," his father
    said.
"You rose each time you fell."

III

And now when things seem dark
    and hard
And difficult to face,
The memory of that little boy
Helps me in my race.

For all of life is like that race,
With ups and down and all.
And all you have to do to win,
Is rise each time you fall.

"Quit! Give up! You're beaten."
They still shout in my face.
But another voice within me says:
"GET UP AND WIN THE RACE!"

Dr D H (Dee) Groberg

WEEK `ONE`:

DEDICATED
HEROES

DEDICATED:

committed, loyal, devoted, single-minded, faithful, wholehearted; devoted to a cause, ideal, or purpose; solemnly given to or set apart for a high purpose; **wholly committed to a purpose or cause;** zealous in loyalty or affection.

HERO:

Someone who is endowed with great courage and strength, **celebrated for his bold exploits;**

a person noted for feats of courage or nobility of purpose;

especially someone who has risked or sacrificed his or her life;

one who endures loss or hardship for others;

a **person noted** for special achievement in a particular field.

> Never give in, never give in, never, never, never, never —
> in nothing great or small, large or petty — never give in
> except to convictions of honour and good sense.
> WINSTON CHURCHILL

> **Obsessed is just a word the lazy use to describe dedicated.**
> UNKNOWN AUTHOR

> **We will either find a way, or make one.**
> HANNIBAL

> **Dreams and dedication are a powerful combination.**
> WILLIAM LONGGOOD

SOMETHING TO LIVE FOR...
... SOMETHING WORTH DYING FOR!

DAY 1

LIVING MY DREAM – JOSEPH

ACTIVATION AND FOCUS:

This is the moment to grasp your deepest desires and begin to turn them into reality. We all carry dreams – often God-inspired – but, like Joseph, we need to keep them in focus. Life rarely makes it easy for us to see our dreams come true, but in the end we need to seize the opportunities we have each day and hold the bigger picture in sight. Joseph did not allow his brothers' betrayal, the injustice of Potiphar's wife, the hardship of prison, or isolation from his family to distract him from his destiny. He made conscious decisions to forgive, be reconciled with, and bless the people in his life for the greater reward of living his God-given dream. Then, when his brothers re-enter his life, he is able to be gracious because he can see the fingerprints of God throughout his life, bringing him to the place where he can LIVE his dream.

> **Genesis 45:7–8**
>
> "But God sent me ahead of you to preserve for you a remnant on earth and to save your lives by a great deliverance.
> "So then, it was not you who sent me here, but God. He made me father to Pharaoh, lord of his entire household and ruler of all Egypt."

I have discovered that it only takes a moment for God to inspire us with a vision, but it takes a lifetime to achieve it. God's plan for fulfilling the dream usually takes us on a very circuitous route – unfortunately there is no "fastest route" on God's GPS! But if we keep our hearts clean and our vision clear we can arrive at our destination looking like champions. The challenge is this: will we let our difficulties provoke us to be more determined to live rooted in God's call, or will we become polluted by negative emotions and reactions?

When Joseph was living on the farm in Israel with his family and had his dream of prominence and leadership, he had no understanding of what the end of the story would look like, but he cherished his dream. He always sought to serve, excelled in all circumstances, and learnt from each apparent setback. He remained spiritually aware throughout his hard experiences and so was ready to interpret the dreams of Pharaoh when called to do so. In the end it was a routine request to interpret another dream that suddenly opened the last door of opportunity for Joseph, enabling him to step into his destiny.

Today as you decide to "run your race", be aware that you do not know what this course will look like, but be determined you

Something to live for...

will run it with excellence. It is better to finish the race with honour and take longer than finish with disgrace. Decide that you will not take any short cuts which sacrifice integrity, but that with God's help you will do what He has called you to achieve. So take a moment to consider what God has called you to be and ensure that your dream has not become ensnared in wrong attitudes and mindsets.

HEARTCRY OF PRAYER:

Today, Father, I want to dedicate my life to You afresh and commit my heart to live with a right attitude. I ask You to help me awaken every vision and dream that I have for my life. Help me to purify my heart from all bitterness, resentment and unforgiveness, especially where I have seen others as unhelpful. Father, where I have become complacent and weary, awaken a new sense of dedication in my life. Speak to me again and stir my sense of purpose and vision. Let me live my dream. Thank You, Father. Amen.

DAY 2
YOUNG, GIFTED, BUT EXCLUDED – DAVID

ACTIVATION AND FOCUS:

David had outstanding gifts but was overlooked. When David's destiny was confirmed by the prophet Samuel, even his father Jesse was not aware of the calling of kingship on David's life. When Jesse had been asked to line up all

> ⌃ **1 Samuel 18:14–15**
> In everything he did he had great success, because the LORD was with him. When Saul saw how successful he was, he was afraid of him.

his sons, he left David in the fields, considering him too young and inexperienced for such an occasion. Yet God made sure he was noticed and brought him into the correct place to receive his blessing. Later, when David was sent with food for his brothers to the battle lines where Israel was fighting the Philistines, his brother Eliab was not impressed. As David began to ask questions Eliab publicly ridiculed him, calling him conceited. When David then said he wanted to go and fight Goliath, Saul was not encouraging either, dismissing David as "just a boy" with little experience. David, however, was not offended but rather determined to be obedient to God.

David did not let the hostile atmosphere and lack of affirmation from his family cause him to stumble. He kept on rehearsing the faithfulness of God as each opposition came against him, and he stood with courage and determination. Once he had overcome Goliath, having had to face the battle alone, he was suddenly cheered as a hero and surrounded by new "friends"! In an instant he went from being unnoticed to being the most popular boy in town. However, fame has its price too. Very soon this popularity was noticed by King Saul, who was not amused that David was stealing his limelight and became jealous. Now David was excluded and threatened all over again.

David was not always loved and accepted, but he still did what he was called to do. Do not let your desire for popularity rob your destiny. You, like David, will have to learn to win this battle in your mind. People may not like you today, but it does not necessarily mean that you are wrong – indeed, later they may turn and love you, and you will need to be ready to embrace them.

Often as we step out to fulfil our calling, we are misunderstood by our family, friends and leaders. We can feel isolated. But if we are to be those who pursue our purpose, we will have to learn to win the popularity battles that plague our minds. People may accuse you of being proud, or be jealous of your favour and success, but in these moments it takes determination to hold fast to your calling and persevere. Remember God will always ensure that He gets you to the right place at the right time if you trust Him. We do not need to push or promote ourselves – God is able to help you succeed and fulfil His desire for your life. So rest, listen to what God says about your future, and do not be alarmed if you feel excluded by those who should help you at this stage of life.

HEARTCRY OF PRAYER:

Jesus, I am so grateful that You hold the keys of my life in Your hands. I trust You that You will always provide an open door for me at the right time, even when I feel isolated and unable to accomplish what I have been called to do. Help me to hear You clearly. Direct me so that I know what I should do in this season of my life, and give me strength to do it even if I seem to be alone. Just like David had Samuel in his life to strengthen him, I pray that You will also give me divine connections to help me know what I should do and where I should go. Father, help me to win the popularity battle in my mind and above all to know that You love me deeply. Thank You. Amen.

DAY 3 DISTINCTIVELY DIFFERENT– DEBORAH

ACTIVATION AND FOCUS:

Often the passion with which we carry our vision can appear obsessive or strange to other people. They cannot understand why it is so demanding, requires our money, and occupies so much thinking time. The call of God is rarely convenient or expected. Recently, I met a woman who went on a much needed beach holiday to Goa. She had just completed a long-term teaching post in a challenging school and was exhausted. She imagined a time of relaxation, reading her favourite novels, and enjoying the sun. But once she arrived on the beaches of Goa, God captivated her and gave her a vision for the street children there, and her holiday became a mission. She now dedicates her time to educating and fundraising for the street kids of Goa.

> **Judges 5:7**
> "Village life in Israel ceased, ceased until I, Deborah, arose, arose a mother in Israel."

Deborah felt the need to arise and do something extraordinary. She was called to lead her nation in a time of crisis and it required her to take unusual action. She had to break the mould of cultural expectations and not be afraid to be different. She needed to be ready to lead as a woman in the midst of a society that expected men to lead. But she knew she was called and so she rose up. Her culture told her she could not lead: not only was she female, but she neither came from nor married into one of the elite families, so she had no natural reason to believe that she could make a difference. However, she herself knew she was called to arise and break the oppression that was destroying her nation.

Today it still takes courage to go against peer pressure and the expectations of society. We do not want to stand out and be considered fanatical and weird. But Deborah knew she was called to do something different and bring change. She was ordinary, but she let the extraordinary God "upgrade" her ability to make a difference in her community. Throughout history there have been many who have had to take a stand and be considered strange in order to change public opinion. Individuals such as William Wilberforce, who said "Not on my watch" and challenged mindsets concerning slavery, and finally managed to abolish the laws which had allowed the slave trade. These determined heroes of change did not have access to the largest bank accounts, the best intellect or greatest charisma but they each had a cause of justice and the determination that they needed to rise up.

History makers have this unique quality of being fearlessly different from the norm. They are ready to take a stand in their day, be different, and bring transformation. We too need to be ready to arise, carry our distinct vision and lead. Our cry may irritate those conditioned by the "live and let live" mentality of our society, but it is necessary to awaken the sleeping majority to the fact that change must happen. We must see family life restored, marriage honoured, unborn babies rescued, the sex traffickers stopped and

... something worth dying for!

Something to live for...

injustice prevented. But it needs a person who is not afraid to live a distinctively different life. Will that be you?

HEARTCRY OF PRAYER:

Father, help me live free from the fear of what other people think about me. Let me be one who is ready to rise up and be different. Let me have the courage to live a different way and set higher standards. Help me identify where peer pressure controls my attitudes and actions. I know I have a cry for justice so help me stand up and speak clearly about what matters to me. Teach me to arise and stand for my beliefs and not just merge with the consensus of opinion. Help me step forward and shake off all fear. Thank You. Amen.

DAY 4 — GOT IT WRONG – AGAIN! – PETER

ACTIVATION AND FOCUS:

What a relief it is to realize that you do not have to be perfect to birth your dreams. We would expect Peter to stand up and be distinctively different like Deborah; yet he hides and denies any association with Jesus. Here is Peter, one of the greatest men of the Bible, called to follow Jesus

> **Matthew 16:17–18**
>
> Jesus replied, "Blessed are you, Simon son of Jonah, for this was not revealed to you by man, but by my Father in heaven. And I tell you that you are Peter, and on this rock I will build my church, and the gates of Hades will not overcome it."

and build the church, yet he buckles under fear when challenged by those who hate Jesus. How wonderful it is to know that God is able to handle our repeated mistakes, and help us to overcome them and still birth our dreams. I like Peter; he is passionate and expressive but often gets it wrong. I also like Peter because he does not give up; he learns from his mistakes and becomes a fine leader. Peter has an amazing revelation of the Christ, immediately followed by an ungodly emotional reaction. One moment he is speaking with divine revelation and the next he is responding in anger and then fear. We need to learn that, as with Peter, our mistakes do not disqualify us from eventual accomplishment. Success can build character but failure often reveals it. So do

Something to live for...

not fear making mistakes but realize that true failure is just not learning from them. Allow God to teach you His way of success and learn on the job.

In fact, most people who eventually leave a significant legacy have had their catalogue of failures on the way. Nearly every successful invention we know today had its financial challenges or disasters in its early days. Thomas Edison held 1,093 patents for different inventions. Many of them, such as the light bulb and the motion picture camera, were brilliant creations that now have a huge influence on our everyday life. However, not everything he created was an immediate success – some things initially failed. He formed the Edison Portland Cement Co. in 1899, and made everything from houses to pianos in cement. Unfortunately, at the time, concrete was too expensive so the idea was never accepted – it was considered his huge failure. Time has changed this failure into success!

A Chinese proverb says, "True failure is not falling down but falling down and then refusing to get up." Like Peter, we must learn to look at our failures as stepping stones on the way to fulfilling God's plan in our lives. Remember, now is a time to arise and dream again. Consider setbacks with fresh perspective and see times of disappointment as springboards into the next season. I remember that when I failed one exam, which was a final requirement for medical school, I felt so devastated and was convinced I was a failure. Depression began to grip me until a friend spoke some truth to me: "Rachel," he said, "you may have failed but that does not make you a failure!" So take a moment to read the poem, "Get up and win the race" at the front of this book and decide, whatever the hindrances, you will arise and RUN YOUR RACE.

HEARTCRY OF PRAYER:

Father, help me look at the difficult seasons of disappointment with new eyes. So often I see failure and then consider myself a failure – instead help me understand the lessons to be learnt and the changes to be made. Teach me to see Your hand training me in the midst of trials. Thank You for Your patience with me. Thank You that even in my mistakes You can show me my future and help me win the race. Help me rise up and take my place again. Thank You, God. Amen.

DAY 5 DETERMINED NOT TO BE ALONE – RUTH

ACTIVATION AND FOCUS:

Sometimes we find ourselves in a place of difficulty through no fault of our own. Recently I was sitting with a gifted woman who was describing the last five years of her life. She had watched her family face divorce, death, sickness, financial injustice, and betrayal, and she finally concluded that she could not believe she was in this

> **Ruth 1:16**
>
> But Ruth replied, "Don't urge me to leave you or to turn back from you. Where you go I will go, and where you stay I will stay. Your people will be my people and your God my God."

position. "How did I get here?" she exclaimed. "This was not on my wish list!" I am sure Ruth could identify. Ruth had married a good man, watched him die, then lost her father-in-law, and now her mother-in-law was leaving her too. However, Ruth knew she could not let her circumstances dictate her future. She kept focused on the bigger picture. When Naomi came to say farewell, Ruth would not let her go. Even though Naomi did her best to shake free of her relationship with Ruth, Ruth would not let go. Ruth could see a greater purpose through all the pain. She knew that Naomi was part of her future and destiny and she wanted to maintain this relationship in spite of all the painful memories that would be triggered by it. Now determination gripped Ruth and she would not let go. We read in the book of Ruth, chapter 1 and verse 18 that, "When Naomi realized that Ruth was determined to go with her, she stopped urging her." Ruth had made her famous statement of commitment, "where you go I will go", and Naomi now knew this was one determined lady. She would not take no for an answer. She was coming!

Ruth realized she could not step into her destiny alone and so refused to let Naomi's bitterness and rejection rob her of their relationship. Ruth had the courage to speak out and so gained the wise advice of someone familiar with the decisions she would go on to face. So often the enemy tries to disconnect us from the people we need in life, who can help us fulfil our vision. We need the wisdom of this older generation to win. As you come to step into your destiny be aware of the relational challenges that will arise. The way you handle these times of crisis is vital. Often, due to the painful memories, we just want to leave and create distance between our lives and difficult issues. We want to retreat, move far away and forget. However, we must hold our ground, work through the memories, and conquer our fears. We cannot fulfil our purpose as isolated robots devoid of relationship. We must remain open and vulnerable, even towards those who remind us of the pain. Ruth stepped into her future but not away from the challenge. Once Ruth was rightly positioned

... something worth dying for! 33

Something to live for...

the rest of her story unfolded: she found her second husband, gave birth to a son, made Naomi a happy grandmother, and became part of the generational legacy of Jesus. Wow, what a good choice she made to keep connected to the last generation!

HEARTCRY OF PRAYER:

Lord, please help me make the right choices in this season. Even when it would appear easier to move on and just erase the difficult memories of past relationships, show me which people and places should still be part of my future. Help me be wise and handle each relationship with grace. Father, show me where I have become isolated and try to live my life alone. Teach me how to trust others to direct me. Father, let me be one who partners with the generations to bring a greater blessing to those around me. Help me be faithful in my commitments and serve them even when it is tough. Thank You, Father. Amen.

DAY 6 UNCERTAIN DESTINATION – ABRAHAM

ACTIVATION AND FOCUS:

Uncertainty is never a comfortable feeling. Taking big risks has never been one of my natural gifts. I like to make thorough risk assessments before I leap, yet I have discovered that God frequently asks us to jump when we cannot see the future clearly. I

> **Hebrews 11:8**
> By faith Abraham, when called to go to a place he would later receive as his inheritance, obeyed and went, even though he did not know where he was going.

remember when God asked us to give away our entire savings fund to a pastor who needed a new car, leaving us with no spare cash for any crisis. Although it was a big step of faith, I knew God had challenged us to a new level of generosity and I needed to obey. So I walked to the pastor's house with my baby in the pram and gave the gift to the couple. I "jumped" in faith, and gave, but now wondered what we would do if we needed money. A crisis did come and the finance seemed slow in arriving, but just when I began to doubt our decision to give, God provided the money we required and since that time He has more than supplied our every need. God often directs us to go without telling us the final destination, and we just have to respond without knowing where we are going or where we will end up! These are the adventures on the journey of birthing your dreams.

In this verse Abraham was told to take his extended family, leave everything that was familiar, and travel to a new land where his inheritance would be revealed. It takes great trust to step out and begin to move before you understand the full picture. Often you have to start to explore your "Promised Land" before you know where you are going or how God's promises will be fulfilled. Abraham had a clear promise that he and his wife, Sarah, would have children, but the facts showed that they were both barren. The future seemed impossible and the path uncertain. However, Abraham did not let his future be defined by these facts, but rather by God's promises. He took hold of these words, which he knew to be the truth, and wrestled with them in faith until the evidence of his barrenness yielded to the truth of God's promise. God's truth will always outlive the facts. Whatever your bank balance shows today, hold fast to the promise of God's provision. Whatever the doctor's report says about your health, carry with confidence His promise of healing. This journey is often difficult, as we have to set out not knowing where the path will take us, but we can know that we will arrive in the land of the goodness of God. So, today, let a new determination spur you into the land of your promises. Even when you cannot see how all the details will work out or if the destination will ever be reached, ask God to show you the way one step at a time and trust Him. If we are ever to be a radical people who achieve our dreams we have to learn to take more risks, and entrust our lives more completely to the goodness of God.

HEARTCRY OF PRAYER:

Father, I know I need to have a greater trust when I cannot see the end from the beginning. Help me trust my uncertain future to a known God. Lord, help me be faithful and answer the challenge of obedience even when it is not easy. Help me make courageous choices and go where You ask me to go. In this season remind me of Your promises and show me how to hold them in faith. Let me grow in faith so that I will see Your answers to these words of truth. Thank You, Jesus. Amen.

Something to live for...

DAY 7 BIG DREAMS FOR A CHILD – JESUS

ACTIVATION AND FOCUS:

I do not know if you ever have this sense, but often I feel there is a huge gulf between what I know to be true on the inside of me and what I see evidenced on the outside. The expectations that I carry in my heart are so BIG, but as yet the reality of what I see around me is only a small part of the dream being

> **Luke 2:51–52**
>
> Then he went down to Nazareth with them and was obedient to them. But his mother treasured all these things in her heart. And Jesus grew in wisdom and stature, and in favour with God and men.

birthed. Yet we need to learn to treasure these things in our heart, knowing there will be a day when we will see our dreams in the flesh. In the meantime, we need to hold fast with faith and expectation to the depth and breadth of our longings and not let them be diluted or downsized.

Here we read that Mary watched Jesus and, although to others He looked ordinary, she knew that He was extraordinary. She hid all this expectation in her heart and waited. Others may have felt He was "old beyond his years", but she knew there would be a time when all would be revealed. As she silently observed her son, Jesus continued to grow in character and opportunity making the right choices to align Himself with both God and men so that at the right time He would be in the

right place with the right attitude, ready to act.

Waiting with determined patience for the right time to birth your dreams is so difficult. Often we distract ourselves with other pastimes or relationships, seeking to diminish the sense of urgency we feel concerning the projects that we are carrying. But Jesus was able to carry the responsibility of His call with wisdom and maturity, even as a twelve-year-old child. God often calls us when we are young but then does not release us until later. These waiting seasons can be frustrating and need to be navigated with sensitivity and maturity beyond our natural years. I was four years old when I gave my life to Jesus, seventeen years old when I was called to the ministry, twenty-four years old when I went to the mission field but thirty years old before I began to preach and minister, thirty-four years old when I founded Heartcry, and forty-five years old when I wrote my first book. All this time I knew I was called but I went through various stages of desire, terror, reluctance, horror, frustration, joy, and difficulty.

Childhood dreams are important – even if you were not saved until later in life, do not despise those early days of dreaming. Maybe the context of your life ambitions is now different, but the deep desires and focus of your life remain similar. I have met many people who say to me, "When I was a child I always wanted to be a musician, but I was not saved so what should I do now?" Often, when encouraged, they become vital parts of our worship, songwriting or other creative arts teams. Others have said, "I wanted to go into business and make money", so once saved they

can use this same gift to bless others through their generosity. Childhood imagination is important, so take time to remember those dreams of your youth and treasure them.

HEARTCRY OF PRAYER:

Father, awaken the longings of my early years. Heal me where my confidence has been so damaged that I cannot believe these desires can be part of my life now. Increase in me wisdom and maturity so that I can hold fast to these dreams with faith-filled determination, knowing You have called and gifted me in these areas. Thank You, Father, for showing me that with dedication I can accomplish what You have placed within me. Help me nurture these desires with Your wisdom and in Your timing. Thank You. Amen.

WEEK TWO:

DETERMINED
COURAGE

DETERMINED

resolute, firm, dogged, fixed, constant, bold, intent, persistent, relentless, stalwart, persevering, single-minded, purposeful, tenacious, undaunted, strong-willed, steadfast, unwavering, immovable, unflinching, strong-minded; one who devotes full strength and concentrated attention towards their cause; **someone who is strongly motivated to succeed;** this person has made a firm decision.

COURAGE

bravery, nerve, fortitude, **boldness**, resolution, daring, grit, heroism, mettle, **firmness**, gallantry, valour; the state or quality of mind or spirit that enables one to face danger or fears with self-possession, confidence, and resolute bravery; the confidence to act in accordance with one's beliefs.

> That man who has never been in danger
> cannot answer for his courage.
> DUC DE LA ROCHEFOUCAULD [MAXIMS]

> Sometimes even to live is
> an act of courage.
> SENECA [LETTERS TO LUCILIUS]

Real leaders are ordinary people with extraordinary determination.
UNKNOWN AUTHOR

Courage is not simply one of the virtues but the form of every virtue at the testing point.
C. S. LEWIS

SOMETHING TO LIVE FOR...
... SOMETHING WORTH DYING FOR!

DAY 8 COURAGE THAT IS UNASHAMED

ACTIVATION AND FOCUS:

When I see the word courage I have two reactions: I immediately think of all the amazing people who have shown outstanding courage as they lived their dream and also wonder if I have the same qualities. When confronted by tough decisions, will I make the courageous choice? I remember my husband, Gordon, making the decision to tell his parents he was leaving the army, their dream for his life, and going as a missionary to Africa. When Jesus becomes the passion of your life it redefines your priorities. It can become difficult to articulate this to people who do not understand the depth of your relationship with God. The media, institutions, and sometimes friends can react to this "fanatical" lifestyle and as a result we can feel forced to hide our faith away from the hostile public glare. But courage needs to be lived and expressed. We need to break free from this cloud of suspicion and mockery, and clearly state that we are not ashamed of Jesus nor of His values and morals. It always takes courage to

 Romans 1:16

I am not ashamed of the gospel, because it is the power of God for the salvation of everyone who believes: first for the Jew, then for the Gentile.

 2 Timothy 1:12

That is why I am suffering as I am. Yet I am not ashamed, because I know whom I have believed, and am convinced that he is able to guard what I have entrusted to him for that day.

make this stand.

A friend of mine said recently, "If God meant us to have courage… why did he give us legs?" I understand that feeling of wanting to be brave but, when faced with opposition, just wanting to run. So what is courage? One writer states that true courage is never letting your actions be influenced by your fears. As you run your race of life you know that God is asking you to speak with greater boldness. It is time for us to declare without fear that we believe Jesus is good news for our nation. We are not ashamed of the Bible and believe that it is relevant for life today. We are not ashamed to say that we believe true marriage is between a man and a woman, and is a blessing from God. We need to shake off the cloak of apology and shame to bravely speak of our affection for Jesus.

I remember being ridiculed while at boarding school in India for my love for God. But I made the choice to speak. At first it caused even greater isolation and bullying, but slowly girls began to find me and ask questions. Soon we were having prayer meetings in the school and many girls came to Jesus – but first I had to break

Something to live for...

the sound barrier of intimidation and find my voice. Then I returned to the UK and began to work at St Bartholomew's Hospital. Here I struggled to find my "sound" as the hostile atmosphere towards God felt overwhelming. But another girl, Angela, joined the staff and as she spoke out I found my voice!

I loved this quote by Andrew Jackson, the seventh president of the USA, that I read recently: "One man with courage makes a majority." So it is time to stand and speak without shame about what really matters to us. Let a courageous generation arise!

HEARTCRY OF PRAYER:

Today, Father, forgive me for the times when I have felt ashamed of my relationship with You. Give me a new boldness and wisdom to speak about You to others. Help me strengthen others around me who find it hard to talk about Jesus. Show me where I need to deal with the fears that stifle my voice and limit my actions. Teach me to live life with courage and openness about my love for You! Thank You. Amen.

DAY 9 ASTONISHING COURAGE

ACTIVATION AND FOCUS:

Astonishing courage is a hallmark of ordinary people who are connected with Jesus. I love this Scripture. People knew the natural character and ability of Peter and John, so when they saw the remarkable courage shown by these two men they knew Jesus had enabled Peter and John to become extraordinary. As a child I loved to read missionary stories of brave people who lived daring lives of faith due to their total commitment to God. Today, as you consider your life, remember that, even though YOU are ordinary, GOD will enable you to live an extraordinary life.

 Acts 4:13

When they saw the courage of Peter and John and realized that they were unschooled, ordinary men, they were astonished and they took note that these men had been with Jesus.

However, when we are in a moment that requires great courage, we often do not realize the sense of bravery we demonstrate to the bystanders around us. They watch our lives and are astonished by our courage. In Malaysia, over twenty years ago, God asked us to organize an outreach with Reinhard Bonnke in the city of Kuala Lumpur. The church leaders were fearful that, with an Islamic government and having just had ten members of Youth With A Mission arrested for street evangelism, we would go to prison. So we prayed but felt all the more strongly that this was right. We encountered various setbacks but as we prayed, again and again God opened the doors of impossibility. God enabled us to hire the Merdeka Stadium, the national sports stadium which hosted the Southeast Asian Games, as the venue for this event. Then all the permits and the visas necessary for these meetings were released and we hosted a six-day gathering. Although we were aware that what we were doing was risky, we had no idea it was so dangerous.

Later in life I met some of our friends from Malaysia who told us they thought we had "astonishing courage". Did we not realize we could have been arrested? Sent to jail? Did I not worry for Gordon and our two young children? At the time I remember thinking of some of these scenarios but then just feeling such peace to continue. I realize that as we stayed in the place of prayer God gave us His courage. I was not aware that I was being given grace to walk through this time of danger, but God had given me extraordinary courage. This is the strange quality of courage – you do not realize you have it until you need it, and even then others recognize it more than you do yourself!

I have watched many amazing people with extraordinary courage. These are the people who face bankruptcy and find faith to start their business all over again; lose a child in tragic circumstances and then start a children's home to help the poor; lose a leg in an accident and then work in the community to help prisoners. These are people of great courage. But I am often

surprised: the person I thought would be strong and cope with the trauma of learning they had cancer has crumpled, while someone I would have considered more needy has flourished, found courage and been resilient throughout. Often it is only the tough times that reveal our true resources. It was obvious that the contemporaries of Peter and John were surprised at their ability to show courage.

Something to live for...

It was unexpected. But because they had the right connections with Jesus they were able to flourish in difficulty.

So do not fear tough times, worrying that you will not have the courage to face the pain, but instead just stay connected to Jesus and you will display astonishing courage.

HEARTCRY OF PRAYER:

Father, I thank You that You can make me extraordinary even when I feel ordinary. Please enable me to stand with courage as I face challenging circumstances and to know You will never leave me alone. Thank You for Your grace to excel at all times. Let me grow deeper in my relationship with You so that people will recognize that I have been with Jesus. Amen.

DAY 10 | TAKE COURAGE!

We admire people of outstanding courage, but then evaluate our capabilities and disqualify ourselves from their noble ranks! Instead, today hear Jesus speaking to you. Jesus does not ask us to find courage, develop courage, or even earn courage. In the first passage of Scripture Jesus challenges us to TAKE courage. Often we are so self-reliant that we want to find our own supply of strength to prevail, but here God simply instructs us – TAKE it! Today, as you face decisions and dreams and feel overwhelmed, look into the face of Jesus and take courage for the days ahead.

 Matthew 14:27

But Jesus immediately said to them: "Take courage! It is I. Don't be afraid."

Acts 23:11

The following night the Lord stood near Paul and said, "Take courage! As you have testified about me in Jerusalem, so you must also testify in Rome."

Recently I visited a friend who had just been diagnosed with cancer and was about to start a lengthy cycle of chemotherapy and radiotherapy. When I chatted with her she was obviously feeling overwhelmed and shared that she did not like hospitals, so she wondered how she would cope with the routine of the coming months. As we prayed I had a picture for her and saw

Jesus squatting down with his arms extended towards her. She was standing about twenty-five metres away and Jesus called her, saying, "Come, I am watching you and will give you all the help you need." As the truth of this picture resonated in her spirit, she suddenly realized all she had to do to receive this help was to run into His arms and rest. We have to learn to position ourselves in the right place to receive. Just take courage!

In the second Scripture we read how Paul needed a new dose of courage. He had already experienced God's goodness helping him speak in Jerusalem, but now he had to go further. Often it is hard to face the same set of circumstances a second time as your past experience reminds you of the struggle. Sometimes ignorance is bliss! It is like that for many mothers with the birth of a second child. You suddenly remember why you never wanted to go into labour again – it takes courage to engage and deliver your baby as you know the pain of the birthing process now. Maybe you have been through a trial of financial difficulty and you survived but now you are facing it again, requiring further courage. Nelson Mandela powerfully expresses the nature of courage:

I learned that courage was not the absence of fear, but the triumph over it. The brave man is not he who does not feel afraid, but he who conquers that fear.

So, know God is with you and just as He helped you previously, He will strengthen you again today. Therefore do not fear the days

ahead but take fresh courage for this season.

Courage to stand for a second time after disappointment requires determination. Winston Churchill said, "Courage is going from failure to failure without losing enthusiasm!" Some may call this stupidity rather than courage but we do need to find the tenacity to try again and not be fearful. Many of us carry a weariness concerning the promises of God for our life and it is easy to just give up, but now is the time to take courage and stand for the second, third and umpteenth time. I feel that in this new season many of the doors of vision that were previously shut

Something to live for...

will now open with brand new opportunities. It is time to knock on those doors of your hopes and dreams and see if they do not open this time round. I was speaking to a pastor several months ago about a project that he wanted to launch in the community. He had tried to raise support two years ago but had no backing or funding released. Yet when I prophesied the same details of this project again, without any prior knowledge of his previous plans, he decided to have another try. This took courage as he had felt so humiliated by the previous lack of response. However, this time it was different – the doors flew open and now he has the buildings and funding necessary to fulfil the mission. SO TAKE COURAGE!

HEARTCRY OF PRAYER:

Father, today, let me see Your face and hear Your voice encouraging me to TAKE COURAGE. Jesus, where I have lost sight of You helping me to stand when I have felt weary I ask You now to give me fresh courage. Give me hope to stand a second time and believe again where I feel I have previously failed. Thank You, God, that You have the courage I need today. Teach me to be a good receiver and take what I need from You. Thank You, Father. Amen.

DAY 11
BE STRONG
– BE COURAGEOUS!

ACTIVATION AND FOCUS:

In a time of change you need to have a vibrant partnership of strength and courage working together in your life. Each of these Scriptures was given to a man of God just as he was about to step out, take hold of his inheritance and make his dream a reality. In their time of transition God encourages each of them to be strong and courageous, and to resist all fear and discouragement. So when change comes make sure you pack lots of courage and strength for the journey! In life I have discovered that it is easier to articulate and define a vision than it is to establish the dream – this is what takes courage and resilience. Usually, as soon as you begin to vocalize your desires, a

Deuteronomy 31:6

"Be strong and courageous. Do not be afraid or terrified because of them, for the LORD your God goes with you; he will never leave you nor forsake you."

Joshua 1:9

"Have I not commanded you? Be strong and courageous. Do not be terrified; do not be discouraged, for the LORD your God will be with you wherever you go."

1 Chronicles 28:20

David also said to Solomon his son, "Be strong and courageous, and do the work. Do not be afraid or discouraged, for the LORD God, my God, is with you. He will not fail you or forsake you until all the work for the service of the temple of the LORD is finished."

2 Chronicles 32:7

"Be strong and courageous. Do not be afraid or discouraged because of the king of Assyria and the vast army with him, for there is a greater power with us than with him."

thousand problems materialize and make your plans seem absurd. So then you have to be strong and hold fast to what you know God has asked you to do. The Bible constantly challenges the heroes of our faith to stand, be strong, and take hold of their inheritance. Remember, when the season of inheritance comes so does the time for courage. Everything will rise against us to discourage us and push us back, but we need to hold fast to our convictions with fresh determination and press through to obtain our promises.

Sometimes courage requires us to think outside the box and take a bold step. I live in Oxford and often hear stories about the fierce competition to get a place at the university. Here is one story that illustrates this point: 280 students had reached the final selection for the 8–10 available places to study PPE (Philosophy, Politics and Economics) at one of the Oxford colleges. They had been invited to attend three days of further selection at the college and one requirement was to write a three-hour exam on any subject from the three disciplines to be given on the day. On entering the hall the students turned over their papers and read the essay title. "What is courage? Discuss." One essay, three hours. One boy sat and thought, then after an hour wrote two words, handed back his paper to the examiner and left the hall. The tutor was surprised – then he read the answer, and smiled. The student had written as an answer to the question "What is courage?", "THIS IS!", and then walked out! The boy got his place! Often if we are to possess our place of destiny we have to take brave decisions to get there. So today consider where you need to be strong and courageous

and stand against all that would terrify or discourage you. This is your time to run your race and win with courage and bravery.

Father, where I have allowed fear and discouragement to control my life I ask You to help me exchange them for strength and courage. I know that if I am going to do what You have called me to do, I need to stand more boldly on my promises. Give me the strategy to take hold of all You have placed in my heart. Let me know what I should do to take hold of these promises in my life. Partner me with people who can help me fulfil my dreams and strengthen my resolve and vision. Thank You, Father. Amen.

COURAGE TO SAY NO!

DAY 12

ACTIVATION AND FOCUS:

We are in a spiritual battle and now is the time to courageously stand and not yield to the pressure of moral tolerance. At this time so many standards are being shaken and challenged, but we need to have the courage of our convictions and speak out. In the book of Joshua, we are promised that every place where the soles of our feet tread will be given to us. We need to put our foot down in the areas of justice and integrity. If we move our feet away from the gates of education, medicine, justice, the media, and social welfare in our nation we will lose our voice of Christian influence. This is a battle for the moral fibre of our nation and we need to make a courageous stand.

> **Ephesians 6:11–14**
>
> Put on the full armour of God so that you can take your stand against the devil's schemes. For our struggle is not against flesh and blood, but against the rulers, against the authorities, against the powers of this dark world and against the spiritual forces of evil in the heavenly realms. Therefore put on the full armour of God, so that when the day of evil comes, you may be able to stand your ground, and after you have done everything, to stand. Stand firm then…

In definitions of courage, a distinction is often made between moral and physical courage. "Physical courage" is defined as courage shown in the face of physical pain, hardship, or threat of death, while "moral courage" is the courage needed to act rightly in the face of popular opposition, shame, scandal, or discouragement.

Mark Twain makes this powerful statement, "It is curious that physical courage should be so common in the world and moral courage so rare." This quote should be a provocation to the church. In this day of suicide bombings and other extreme acts that, although misguided, require great bravery, the church, in contrast, has grown silent concerning the standards of moral integrity. We need to realize that we are not just fighting the opinions of society or cultural attitudes, but that keeping this moral ground is a spiritual battle. We need to clearly identify the battle zones and then courageously sound the battle cry and speak out. We must not get caught in the trap of personalities and hate campaigns, but instead recognize we are dealing with spiritual agendas that want to reform the Christian foundations of our society. This is a time to say NO and hold our ground.

Something to live for...

I am so grateful for the forerunners who have stood in our nations to battle for justice and integrity, but we need a new generation of courageous reformers who will stand and speak for truth. We need lawyers who will courageously represent those isolated for their stand of faith. We need people who will expose those involved with drug deals, sex trafficking, and crimes against children. We need an army of courageous people who will say NO to the slipping standards of our morality.

HEARTCRY OF PRAYER:

Today I ask You to show me where I need to put my feet down and seek to see Your righteousness established. Help me discern the atmospheres in my neighbourhood and workplace that are undermining Your standards of justice and morality. Give me a new courage to speak out about injustice and show me what I can  practically do to make a difference. Help me make a stand and go with the courage of my convictions. Amen.

DAY 13 SILENT COURAGE

As we are reminded in Ecclesiastes 3:7, there is "a time to be silent and a time to speak". Although we must take our stand and speak out concerning standards of morality, there are also times when courage requires silence. Winston Churchill made this observation: "Courage is what it takes to stand up and speak; courage is also what it takes to sit down and listen." It takes courage to sit and listen to correction, but it often requires greater courage to listen to criticism, identify the threads of truth and then respond correctly. It takes the silent strength of conviction to separate truth from accusation and to hold fast to the right words. Like most of us, I have had conversations that have increased my resolve to press forward, and others that have just confused me. We need to decide to tune our ears with discernment to constructive words but resist all false accusation.

> ⌃ **Acts 7:55**
>
> But Stephen, full of the Holy Spirit, looked up to heaven and saw the glory of God, and Jesus standing at the right hand of God.
>
> ⌃ **Acts 27:22,25**
>
> But now I urge you to keep up your courage, because not one of you will be lost; only the ship will be destroyed... So keep up your courage, men, for I have faith in God that it will happen just as he told me.

In Joshua 2:11 we read, "When we heard of it, our hearts sank and everyone's courage failed because of you, for the LORD your God is God in heaven above and on the earth below." We have already seen that fear and discouragement are enemies of the strong and courageous, so it is in the silent places of the heart that our courage must conquer. Every project or dream that is God-inspired will be too big for us to fulfil with our own resources. It will always feel impossible but we must see the bigger picture through the eyes of courage. God will help us! In the silent place listen to the assurance of God's promise not the battle in your mind.

In the verses above we read how firstly Stephen and then Paul had courage in a time of crisis. Stephen was about to be martyred for his faith but he focused on heaven. The Scriptures say his face shone like an angel! In his moment of challenge he found a deep, silent peace that enabled him to conquer every fear of death and so he died with courage. If we are to live as people of courage we need to triumph in the secret, quiet places of our hearts and minds so that we will remain strong. Paul was also able to stand firm in a time of trouble. His ship had just been wrecked and everyone feared that they would drown, but he was able to speak from a place of strength to encourage them.

In 2011 we watched uprisings in the Middle East change the political landscape. As the troubles erupted in Egypt, precious Christians decided this was the time for them to show courage. They had been praying for many years, but in February 2011 felt it was the time to join others in the now famous Tahrir (Freedom) Square for a service of dedication. As worship leaders took their guitars onto the square to join the youth they asked God for a sign. They asked God to let it rain while they worshipped. (It does not usually rain in Cairo.) They knew that holding a public act of worship in the square was still illegal and that they could face prison. But they took courage and went. They sang songs about the precious land of Egypt and blessed their nation. Then they sang the song "Let it rain". Two hours later it began to rain and forty-eight hours later it was still wet and cloudy. Their hidden courage of years was now being displayed publicly!

HEARTCRY OF PRAYER:

Father, give me the grace to listen to words that will stir courage within my heart. Help me discern the negative words that will cause me discouragement and resist them. Teach me to be one who gives encouragement to others and helps them overcome troubles. Amen.

DAY 14 PREVAILING COURAGE

ACTIVATION AND FOCUS:

You are made to overcome and obtain your promises. Too often we feel that the promises of God are like carrots dangled out in front of our lives to motivate us to be good, but that will always move just beyond our reach. This is not the true picture. However, it does take courage to keep believing during extended times of delay. As expressed in this thought by Mary Anne Radmacher, "Courage doesn't always roar. Sometimes courage is the quiet voice at the end of the day saying, 'I will try again tomorrow.'"

Asa needed the trigger of this prophetic word to stir his determination to see something change in the landscape of his nation. These words prompted him to take a stand, so he removed the idols from the land, and was motivated to re-establish a godly lifestyle. Today take a moment to remember some of the prophetic words that you have received and let them stir you to fresh hope and action.

 2 Chronicles 15:8

When Asa heard these words and the prophecy of Azariah son of Oded the prophet, he took courage. He removed the detestable idols from the whole land of Judah and Benjamin and from the towns he had captured in the hills of Ephraim. He repaired the altar of the LORD that was in front of the portico of the LORD's temple.

1 John 4:4

You, dear children, are from God and have overcome them, because the one who is in you is greater than the one who is in the world.

God is able to speak to you and help you overcome every obstacle, and get you to the right place at the right time. Here is a testimony from Brenda,

It started when you came to Oregon in May and spoke at our women's conference. It has been tight financially for us this past year but my husband encouraged me to go. I did go, and the words you spoke were everything I needed to hear. But when you shared that you had written a new book called Eat the Word, Speak the Word, *something leapt in me but knew I did not have the money for it. Then I saw you signing the ladies' books and thought I would love you to sign one for me and speak into my life. But I had no money to buy it. Then last week a dear friend came over to spend a couple of days with me and I mentioned to her that you had this new book and she offered to buy one for each of us. That was on Thursday morning. On Thursday evening we were praying for each other and God gave me a direct word for her for this season of her life, and she spoke an encouraging word to me. Well, the very next morning we had to drive to her house to collect something and a box from Heartcry was waiting. Our books from you had arrived the very next day (that is unheard of). We opened the box and I randomly handed my friend a book and took one myself. To our great surprise you had signed both of them. But what you don't know is that the word in each book was identical to the word that we had just spoken to each other the evening before. I don't know when you signed these books but I know God used you to confirm a direct word into our lives and it gave us such hope.*

So today awaken words of prophecy and encourage yourself in His word. God has spoken, He will do it and you will overcome.

HEARTCRY OF PRAYER:

So, Father, I thank You for every word that You have spoken into my life. Give me a new sense of confidence so that I can trust each promise will come forth into reality. Help me overcome every sense of doubt and fear. Give me a new determination that will not let go of Your promises. I receive Your courage to stand and believe that I am made to overcome in the midst of every trouble. Thank You for the courage to see victory even when life is tough. Help me overcome. Amen.

... something worth dying for!

WEEK THREE:
DEVOTED
TO PURITY

DEVOTED

passionate, affectionate, intense, zealous, fervent, adoring;
earnestly committed, loyal, constantly faithful, reverent;
a zealous desire to serve God;
a person who gives their life in faithful, dedicated
affection to a person or principle.

PURITY

clarity, brilliance, genuineness, wholesomeness, innocence,
virtue, integrity, honesty
decency, sincerity, virtuousness, chasteness, blamelessness
free from all dirt, defilement, or pollution;
free from all moral taints;
free from discordant qualities,
a harmonious pure sound.

Your capacity to keep your vow will depend on the level of purity in your life.

MAHATMA GANDHI

To succeed in your mission, you must have single-minded devotion to your goal.

ABDUL KALAM

SOMETHING TO LIVE FOR...
... SOMETHING WORTH DYING FOR!

DAY 15 · PURE TEMPTATION

ACTIVATION AND FOCUS:

None of us starts a day with the desire to fail or make poor choices, but often we can end the day with regrets. Too often gifted people never achieve their potential because they are distracted by things which drain their motivation. Temptation to settle for less than the best beckons to us all. This is your season to win gold, not just to settle for the ordinary, so we have to deal with every enticement that will dilute our devotion to Jesus and His call on our life. I have watched dedicated people, gifted leaders, and amazing ministries settle for less as they get tempted by money, relationships, or reputation. We need to make the hard choice to be devoted with a pure heart to the call upon our lives.

Often we think we are above the lure of temptation and are then surprised when we find ourselves trapped. We often

 Matthew 6:13

"And lead us not into temptation, but deliver us from the evil one."

 Mark 14:38

"Watch and pray so that you will not fall into temptation. The spirit is willing, but the body is weak."

 1 Corinthians 10:13

No temptation has seized you except what is common to man. And God is faithful; he will not let you be tempted beyond what you can bear. But when you are tempted, he will also provide a way out so that you can stand up under it.

 1 Timothy 6:9

People who want to get rich fall into temptation and a trap and into many foolish and harmful desires that plunge men into ruin and destruction.

limit temptation to the challenge of sexual sin and believe we are free from this enticement. Beware – temptation comes dressed in many styles. As this statement by James A. Baldwin expresses so well, "Nobody is more dangerous than he who imagines himself pure in heart; for his purity, by definition, is unassailable." We need to beware when we feel we are through our phase of temptation, and watch and pray! Today, as you consider your call, ask God to show you where your areas of vulnerability are – those areas which could persuade you to downsize your call or pull you away from your devotion to God. Read the Scriptures above again slowly and ask God to show you any snare that is waiting to grip your life.

I remember when Gordon and I knew God was asking us to leave the UK and go to Africa as missionaries. I was battling with the fear of leaving a secure financial base for us and our young children. I had watched God supply our needs again and again as a child (while growing up in India, as the daughter of missionary parents) but now this felt different. I was wrestling with these thoughts as I pushed my pram through the park. Suddenly someone called my name and began to speak to me. In the conversation she suggested that we were leaving for Africa too soon, and that God would never want us to travel when our children were so small. She then proceeded to tell me a story about a family friend who had lost a baby to malaria and urged me to change our decision.

Walking home I felt further panic as I recalled this conversation, but then realized this was a temptation for me to agree with my

fear. Somehow this conversation steeled my resolve and I knew we had to go, and we did. Looking back to those days in Africa, I know they were essential in the formation of the message I carry today. It was such a privilege to work with Reinhard Bonnke – to

learn faith and to see miracles. He challenged me to go for gold and fulfil my call, and also showed me how to resist getting wounded by accusations. He helped me see that God had a call for my life and that I needed to run passionately and obey it with utter devotion. That innocent conversation, dressed in concern, did not look like temptation but it nearly hijacked our call to Africa!

HEARTCRY OF PRAYER:

So, Father, I pray, "lead me not into temptation, but deliver me from the evil one." Father, alert me to every tactic of the enemy to distract, lure, or tempt me. Make me wise to the enemy's plans to hijack my calling. Show me where I could be used, even with the best of intentions, to be a voice of temptation that distracts others. Help me keep a clear motivation in all advice I give to my family and friends. Thank You for keeping my path secure and my purpose clear. Amen.

... something worth dying for!

DAY 16 TOTAL SURRENDER

ACTIVATION AND FOCUS:

Although our calling is important, we must remember that, in our desire to fulfil every God-given purpose, it is not our achievements that will finally count but the depth of our relationship. God loves us and our companionship. We were created for His pleasure and He delights to see our face. Take a moment to read again the definitions of being devoted at the beginning of this chapter. Does your life express affection, intensity, zeal, fervour, adoration, earnestness and commitment in your relationship with God? Are you devoted? In these two psalms we can read of David's devotion to his God. The psalms express intensity and reveal intimacy.

Mother Teresa makes this comment:

 Psalm 86:2

Guard my life, for I am devoted to you. You are my God; save your servant who trusts in you.

 Psalm 27:4

One thing I ask of the LORD, this is what I seek: that I may dwell in the house of the LORD all the days of my life, to gaze upon the beauty of the LORD and to seek him in his temple.

There is always the danger that we may just do the work for the sake of the work. This is where the respect and the love and the devotion come in – remember that we do it to God, to Christ, and that's why we try to do it as beautifully as possible.

If our work is motivated by anything other than our love for God, we could easily become disillusioned and exhausted. We need to keep coming back to the place of worship.

My son loves sports and I often used to watch him train and play. After one match, when the team had won convincingly, the coach first congratulated them on their win, but then reminded them that they must never forget the basics – it was these skills that had helped them win the tournament that day. I believe if we are going to finish like champions we must never forget the basics of our Christian walk. In 1 John 2:14 we read, "I write to you, young men, because you are strong, and the word of God lives in you, and you have overcome the evil one." What is the key to overcoming and finishing our race looking like victors? It will be the result of a life given to the discipline of training our appetites. It will be the time we take to pray, to read the word and to worship. It will be those times that no one knows about where we choose to serve, make a generous offering, or just pray and fast for a situation. It is in these choices that callings are sealed and secured.

So often, when you have the privilege of looking behind the scenes of a successful life, you will find the hallmarks of sacrifice, love, and devotion. True men and women of God take time to invest in the basics of character development and so are able to leave a legacy of honour. When I attend a funeral and listen to the testimonials given by the family, work colleagues, and friends, it is usually the stories of generosity and kindness that leave a lasting impression. Although achievements are vital, it is the character of the person who has fulfilled the tasks that tells the greater story. Finally, consider this thought from a president of the USA, Woodrow Wilson: "You are not here merely to make a living. You are here in order to enable the world to live more amply, with greater vision, with a finer spirit of hope and achievement. You are here to enrich the world, and you impoverish yourself if you forget this task."

HEARTCRY OF PRAYER:

Father, develop in me a new hunger to spend quality time in Your presence. Put in my heart a cry like David's that loves time with You. Help me maintain the secure foundations of character in my life. Help me be devoted to the call You have placed upon my life, but not to lose my affection for You. Teach me to be balanced in my vision for the call and my passion for Your name. Let me be one who is known first and foremost as a lover of Jesus. Amen.

DAY 17   KEEP YOUR WAYS PURE

ACTIVATION AND FOCUS:

We are more aware than ever of the sexual traps that seek to ensnare us and ruin our reputations. We are all aware of secular and church leaders around the world who have made poor sexual choices and so damaged their ability to run their race. In the past we have considered sexual sin to be an exclusively "male problem" but in today's society we must realize that women are no longer immune. With the increase of sexualization, homosexuality, and fantasy in our society we all need to make a determined decision to keep our ways pure!

 Psalm 119:9

How can a young man keep his way pure? By living according to your word.

 Proverbs 15:26

The LORD detests the thoughts of the wicked, but those of the pure are pleasing to him.

 2 Timothy 2:22

Flee the evil desires of youth, and pursue righteousness, faith, love and peace, along with those who call on the Lord out of a pure heart.

As with most sin, we do not realize we have a problem until we recognize it and are prepared to admit that it is one! We can excuse our browsing on the internet as just a "normal guy thing" or our obsession with fantasy novels as "our need to relax after a hard day". But deep within we know when our life is not pure. I remember listening to this challenge: "If your thoughts were to appear on the overhead screen in your church, would you be comfortable if people knew what you were thinking?" This may seem harsh but it is a good reality check. If we are to live devoted lives then our ways need to be pleasing to God. In the Bible it is very clear that God does not enjoy sexual impurity, so we need to change. In the verse above from

Proverbs, you will have read that God detests the thoughts of the wicked, but loves those of the pure. We need to acknowledge that the seeds of sexual sin are first sown in our minds, so we need to take responsibility for and discipline our thoughts.

Often we can feel that lustful thoughts or flirting with pornography are not really affecting our spirituality and that this whole area is overemphasized. It can appear for many years that a secret habit is not limiting your anointing or influence, but do not be fooled. I have found that the enemy loves to keep your sin secret, wait for you to increase in prominence and, just as you are

Something to live for...

about to fulfil your calling, the sin will be exposed, your ministry disqualified, and many people who followed you will be wounded. While your sin is hidden in the dark place it has power over your life but, if confessed, you can walk free and forgiven. The enemy always exposes our secret with maximum humiliation but God always covers our sin with outrageous love. So do not let the devil convince you to live a secret life of compromise. Decide to keep your way pure.

I have had the privilege of praying with many people over the years as they have confessed deep sin and watched the power of forgiveness wash them clean. I have also watched the determination of those who make their lives accountable as they make their vow to keep their way pure. Often we need more than one prayer; we need a friend to walk with us, challenge us, and remind us that we are going to choose to do this right! Today, deal with those little foxes that could ruin your life. Don't make excuses any more but pursue a holy lifestyle free from sexual sin.

HEARTCRY OF PRAYER:

Father, I want my ways to be pleasing to You. Forgive me when I have made excuses for my sin rather than confessing my actions. I ask You to teach me to be pure. Awaken my conscience again so that I do not disregard Your prompting when my choices are challenged. Let all my

thoughts be pleasing to You. Help me recognize when I should run from bad influences and unhelpful friendships. Let me KEEP my ways pure. Amen.

DAY 18   NO MIXED MESSAGES

ACTIVATION AND FOCUS:

One of the meanings of purity that caught my attention is this: to be free from discordant qualities, a harmonious pure sound. There is a pure sound that the church should express. If we are constantly sending mixed messages – speaking about a set of principles and standards but then living differently – we will confuse our friends and family. People need to see that we are dedicated to the cause, not just knowledgeable about it. My daughter, Nicola, had a friend, Marilyn, while at school. When Marilyn was in her late teens she had to make the choice of whether or not to become a professional athlete. At this stage she knew all the information but had to decide if she would pay the price. Would she get up early and train every day? Would she eat the restricted diet? She knew the talk of an athlete, but would she live the life of one too?

One of the greatest contradictions in the church is that we know

 Philippians 2:14–15

Do everything without complaining or arguing so that you may become blameless and pure, children of God without fault in a crooked and depraved generation, in which you shine like stars in the universe…

 Philippians 4:8

Finally, brothers, whatever is true, whatever is noble, whatever is right, whatever is pure, whatever is lovely, whatever is admirable – if anything is excellent or praiseworthy – think about such things.

the talk but we do not always walk the walk. But if we are to be winners we need to do both. The world will be able to understand our devotion to the cause if it is modelled authentically.

It is time for our lives to release a harmonious sound in perfect pitch and get rid of all discordant negativity. Pure sound is so attractive and alluring. When an instrument plays a perfect note or a voice sings in perfect pitch it is captivating. So as we decide to run our race, our devotion needs to echo the distinct sound of our calling. We need to commit ourselves to the task without complaining, and see the finish line as we train and prepare ourselves to win. If you reread the Scriptures above you will note that when the sound is right, so is the response of those around us. Even those who do not understand our life choices will find they respect our faith.

You will note from these Scriptures that our mind needs to be focused on whatever is pure, right, and lovely. What we think about is what we will eventually talk about. If in your free-thinking time you dwell on the possible setbacks and difficulties you could experience, you will find that when you speak you will have a negative perspective on life. Our mouths and minds are closely connected, and what is in our hearts and minds will come out in conversation. So listen to yourself and decide if you need an upgrade in purity. Ask God to give you his perspective on life and decide not to be a negative, discordant sound.

Someone I know, who tended to have a "half empty" perspective on life, cared for her mother at the end of her life.

Something to live for...

Being around her mum more she realized that it was exhausting living around the constant sound of negativity, possible disaster, and caution. Every time she told her mum a story of good news, her mum would retort, "be careful, dear, I am sure it won't last." After caring for her mother for several months, this daughter was frustrated by her mother's constant pessimistic perspective and then realized that her own husband had to live with her! Something happened in that moment of revelation, and this lady transformed her speech. She is now very much a "half full" girl!

HEARTCRY OF PRAYER:

Lord, today let my life release a pure sound of devotion. Show me where I tend to be negative and dwell on the wrong aspects of people and circumstances. Let me be one who sees the good. Help me not to complain or argue about my circumstances. Remove all compromise from my life and let me be a witness to those around me, showing that I do live devoted to You. Thank You, Father. Amen.

DAY 19 — MAINTAINING STANDARDS

When the pressure is on, what short cuts will you use to achieve your goal? Our culture today has a morality that says, "do what you need to do to get where you need to get quickly!" So we will often see cars parked illegally or rubbish dumped on the roadside, or jobs completed without a receipt. We do what is beneficial to us at the time, irrespective of the law or the inconvenience caused to others. We are all devoted to making our life work for us! People who have a strong sense of ethics and morals in the workplace are often begrudgingly respected, but not appreciated. Your commitment to do things "by the book" is a frustration and irritation to those who just want results by any means. It is so easy to get caught in this attitude of life. But will we keep our integrity in the pursuit of our destiny? Will we allow the pressure of budgets, management targets and sales figures to compromise our work ethics? We need to fight to keep our

 Psalm 24:3–4

Who may ascend the hill of the LORD? Who may stand in his holy place? He who has clean hands and a pure heart, who does not lift up his soul to an idol or swear by what is false.

 Titus 1:15

To the pure, all things are pure, but to those who are corrupted and do not believe, nothing is pure. In fact, both their minds and consciences are corrupted.

Something to live for...

integrity intact, so here is some good advice from the founder of an insurance company: "Have the courage to say no. Have the courage to face the truth. Do the right thing because it is right. These are the keys to living your life with integrity." Remember, integrity is doing the right thing even when nobody is watching!

In these Scriptures we can see that our natural instinct will try to blur the edges of purity and alter our standards. When it is left to us to set the moral standards of what is right and wrong, we get it wrong because our consciences and logic can be corrupted and become an unreliable reference point. We need to refer to the "gold standard" of His word and do what God says. We will often find it more time consuming and expensive, but it is better to pay the price than lose your integrity.

I remember a while ago I was parking in a pay and display car park. I had overpaid on my ticket and so when I returned to my car I gave the ticket to someone else, thinking I was being generous by saving them the parking fee. But all the signs in the car park clearly stated that the tickets were not transferable and so what I had done was technically illegal. As I began to consider this, every excuse began to rattle in my head: "Well, everyone does it" – wrong answer! "But I have paid for it so it is not stealing" – WRONG ANSWER! " I was helping someone"… etc! When I went to church that weekend the preacher spoke about generosity and false generosity – when we flatter ourselves we are helping others by breaking the law ourselves. As his illustration, he used the example of non-transferable car park

tickets! I was nailed by the word of God.

So, today, decide in your heart that you will run a righteous race and live by God's rules. No short cuts to the finish line. The pressure to gain power and influence by lowering your standard of righteousness is huge but do not yield. Run your race with purity. Do not lie, cheat, steal, or give a false account of others so that you can look better. Be pure in your intentions and motivations and then, when you finish your race, you will know that you won keeping your faith and integrity intact.

HEARTCRY OF PRAYER:

Father, You know that I desire to run my race with integrity and purity. I want to live my life right and bring honour to You and those I love. Today, I ask You to help me make the right choices when challenged by the peer pressure of my culture. Let me choose your way not the convenient way. Convict me when I try to wriggle out of keeping Your standards. Give me a new integrity in the little things of life. Father, let me be one who has clean hands and a pure heart. Amen.

DAY 20 ROCK SOLID COMMITMENT

ACTIVATION AND FOCUS:

Commitment is a word that frightens many people. They feel unable to commit themselves to any long-term relationship or promise as their trust has been wounded. They often respond by saying, "I don't know what I will be doing from day to day myself, so how can I make this lasting decision?" But in this psalm we read that David asks God to create in him a pure heart and renew a steadfast spirit within him. If we are going to run the race of life well we have to be able to commit for the long haul. God committed himself to us for life and we in turn need to dedicate our life to Him. People who are devoted are able to be committed. So today ask God to renew this steadfast spirit within you.

 Psalm 51:10
Create in me a pure heart, O God, and renew a steadfast spirit within me.

 Proverbs 22:11
He who loves a pure heart and whose speech is gracious will have the king for his friend.

As we run our race we need to be team players who have stable friendships, marriages, and working partnerships. We need to show that we are in these relationships for the long term, and illustrate the language of commitment. We should be those who keep our pledges, promises, guarantees, and word, while our lives model dedication, loyalty, and devotion. These are countercultural

WEEK THREE: DEVOTED TO PURITY

values that may be misunderstood but we need to embrace them. Today friendships often do not last and marriages shatter quickly, but God wants a committed community with strong relationships who will reverse the trend of society. Sometimes our devotion to God is perceived as negative among our non-Christian friends, but once they see our committed lifestyle they often soften. The second Scripture here shows us that even the "king" will be our friend. I believe that when people see the integrity of our relationships it gives them confidence to confide. Initially they may seem suspicious or even mocking of our principles, but as people observe your life and notice that your friendships stand the test of time then people, even prominent people, will trust you with their hearts.

When we were living in Malawi, the Chief Inspector of Police called Gordon to his office. The Chief Inspector informed Gordon that he would have to leave the country, and would never be allowed back, as he was causing too much excitement in the churches with his plans for a National Crusade. But then for no reason, the Inspector asked a question that changed everything: "Why do you people keep coming here? Why do you care about Malawi?" Gordon realized from this question that the Inspector had been watching our relationship with the churches and the people in Blantyre. So Gordon told him that we had a message from God that would address the many problems in the nation. As Gordon continued, the eyes of the Police Chief moistened. Finally he closed his door, got down on his knees and asked Gordon to pray for him. This man reversed his decision, and said to all his staff, "Help these people, they have a message from God for our nation!" Gordon later met him and his wife in a crowd of 150,000: both of them had given their lives to Jesus!

The way we live our lives will challenge even the hostile and turn their hearts towards friendship. Gordon and I have now been married over thirty years. Frequently we are asked, "What is your secret?" Our answer is this – I am committed for life. I have made a decision and as a result I have found the best friend ever!

HEARTCRY OF PRAYER:

Father, as I run my race I pray that You will remove from me all fear of commitment. I am sorry for the times that I have not kept my word to my friends, family, or partner. Help me be someone who is rock solid in my loyalty and commitment. Today, I ask You to work in my life so that I am someone who commits to the long-term dream. Give me opportunities to connect with people of influence as they see my loyalty and work. Thank You for Your grace. Amen.

DAY 21 ZEALOUS FOR PURITY

ACTIVATION AND FOCUS:

When we read the Scripture, "Blessed are the pure in heart, for they shall see God", we could feel discouraged and say, "Well, I am still not pure so I will not see God." But I believe that there is a more positive way to read this verse. "Blessed are the pure in heart": that is, those whose minds, motives, and principles are seeking to have both correct external actions and an internal integrity of heart. People look at outward appearances, but we need to be like God and look at the heart. At the time when this verse was written, people were used to watching the Pharisees and their spirituality, which was all motivated by outward appearances rather than the condition of their hearts. People knew that although the Pharisees acted rightly, their hearts were full of corruption and defilement. They looked "pure" thanks to all their rituals, but their attitude stank! However, God is challenging us that in order to have an intimate, face-to-face friendship with Him, we must guard the wellspring of our heart from all contamination and not just be given to sacrificial activity.

 Matthew 5:8

"Blessed are the pure in heart, for they will see God."

 1 Timothy 1:5

The goal of this command is love, which comes from a pure heart and a good conscience and a sincere faith.

At the beginning of this year I felt God challenge me that if we wanted to see true change in our society then we needed to concentrate on the 3 "C"s of Character, Conscience, and Choice. Here in this second verse we read that our devotion and love will flow out of a pure heart, good conscience and sincere faith. I have been amazed to watch how significant a good choice can be in changing the direction of someone's life. I have sat with precious people, pleading with them to forgive or to reverse a poor decision, but if they will not then there is little one can do to prevent the consequences. However, I have also watched courageous people decide to change and seen the resulting victory in their lives. It is time to be zealous for the right values. Make a good choice today. Why not make your goal one that will set you up for life and success?

I remember sitting with a girl called Gill (not her real name) and listening to her story. She was not yet thirty, but she had lived on the streets, been to jail, been caught doing drugs, and had many other traumatic experiences. As I listened to her, I learned she came from a Christian home and that her father had been a minister. At sixteen she had discovered her father was having an affair, and she went to the leaders of the church and her mum to expose this. She was called a liar and ejected from the church. (Unfortunately she had been a rebellious teenager and so no one took her seriously.) Consequently, her father put her out of the house for being a troublemaker and her life went downhill.

On the evening I spoke to her, she had walked into church and

asked for help, and so we were talking. After hearing her story I asked her if she would forgive her father, the church, and her family for the injustice and pain they had caused. I expected that I would have to convince her this was necessary as I could see she was stubborn. But to my amazement she looked straight at me and said, "Yes — after all, I need lots of forgiveness from God if I am ever to make my life a success after all I have done!" She forgave her dad and I saw her flourish and grow by making this determined choice. As she made love her goal, everything else began to flow!

HEARTCRY OF PRAYER:

Let me make love my goal and teach me to hold fast to a clear conscience, a firm faith, and a pure heart. Let my life have an external and internal balance so that both my actions and my intentions honour You. Father, at the end of this week, I ask You to purify my heart, give me a willingness to forgive, and activate my devotion for You. I want to see You and know You in a deeper way in my life. Father, You are so precious to me. Thank You for loving me. Amen.

WEEK FOUR:

DISCIPLINED
SACRIFICE

DISCIPLINED

Groomed, trained, restrained, showing self-control, able to be corrected, **teachable**;
training expected to produce a specific character or pattern of behaviour, especially training that produces moral or mental improvement;
controlled behaviour resulting from training and **self-control**.

SACRIFICE

To **forfeit one thing of meaning** for another considered to be of greater value;
the surrender of something of value as a means of gaining something more desirable;
to endure the loss of something precious.

> Talent without discipline is like an octopus on roller skates. There's plenty of movement, but you never know if it's going to be forward, backwards, or sideways.
>
> H. JACKSON BROWN, JR

> In this world it is not what we take
> up, but what we give up,
> that makes us rich.
>
> HENRY WARD BEECHER

> Discipline is the bridge between goals and accomplishments.
>
> JIM ROHN

SOMETHING TO LIVE FOR...
... SOMETHING WORTH DYING FOR!

DAY 22 POWER OF A LAID-DOWN LIFE

ACTIVATION AND FOCUS:

The level of discipline and sacrifice you choose to have in your life will determine whether you run your race as a champion or an occasional winner. It is those who make constant choices to give up their personal agenda and train their areas of weakness who grow into people of significance and success. If we lay our life before God and allow Him to train it through the power of the Holy Spirit, extraordinary opportunities become our possibility. God can train the worst sinner

> **Romans 12:1**
>
> Therefore, I urge you, brothers, in view of God's mercy, to offer your bodies as living sacrifices, holy and pleasing to God – this is your spiritual act of worship.

> **Revelation 12:11**
>
> They overcame him by the blood of the Lamb and by the word of their testimony; they did not love their lives so much as to shrink from death.

and make them able to run an exceptional race of destiny. But we need to offer our bodies to the training school of the Holy Spirit. Here the writer of Romans understands this principle and he urges us, "let go of your life and let God take hold of it!" Give up your rights; present yourself as a sacrifice, one ready to endure even the loss of precious things for the sake of the cause. Will you run a race that overcomes every area of your weakness and then triumphs over the enemy's plan in the lives of those around you? Will you run a race that exposes the tactics of the devil and enables you and others to run free? Are you brave enough to live a life of sacrifice?

In today's culture the whole concept of sacrifice, a decision to surrender something valuable as a sign of devotion to God, makes no sense as a key to success in life! People cannot understand the principle of this key: how in giving something away that you value, you will gain even more. Why does the power of denial to yourself in the end promote you to greatness? This is upside-down thinking, but essential for us to understand if we are to be  kingdom-minded. In this quote Aldous Huxley makes a powerful comment: "There's only one effectively redemptive sacrifice, the sacrifice of self-will to make room for the knowledge of God." Will we deny ourselves and let God direct and captivate our lives?

If we find this courage to sacrifice we will gain the power to overcome. In our second Scripture reading we notice that they overcame because they were ready to sacrifice their lives and were not frightened even to die for the cause. Throughout this book you will notice the strapline, "Something to live for... something worth dying for!" This phrase was inspired by a young girl, Abi Ruibal, from Cali, Columbia. When she was a teenager her father

Something to live for...

was martyred for his faith in Columbia. When interviewed she was asked whether she would be prepared to die for her faith too, and she replied, "I want to live for Christ and only if necessary die for Him!" Knowing what she had experienced, I was surprised by the wisdom of this answer from a young teenager who had just lost her dad. Her whole perspective was that she wanted to live for Christ; she wanted to give her life to make a difference. She would not shrink back from the sacrifice of martyrdom if she had to die, but she wanted to do everything to live a meaningful life first. Wow, what courage! What a determined attitude, to sacrifice and offer your life to God, not allowing even tough circumstances to distract you from your calling and pursuit of life. This is the attitude that will enable us to live an overcoming life. This is the power of a laid down life.

HEARTCRY OF PRAYER:

Father, today I lay my life before You. I want to give You my life as a living sacrifice, an offering that will bring You pleasure. Teach me to let go of my agenda, plans, and priorities, and put Your way first. Let me live the life of an overcomer as I choose to allow You to direct my choices. Break every fear of death or humiliation and give me courage to surrender to Your will. Let me learn the keys of discipline and sacrifice. Amen.

DAY 23
WINNING AGAINST MYSELF

ACTIVATION AND FOCUS:

So, provoked by the inspiring stories of people who have paid the price of sacrifice, let us not shrink back from our own challenges. As we read this Scripture, we are challenged to ensure that we train our selfish desires so that we can run through life like a champion. What a cry from the apostle Paul as he urges us to make sure we do not get disqualified by our actions! My son is a keen

> **1 Corinthians 9:25–27**
>
> Everyone who competes in the games goes into strict training. They do it to get a crown that will not last; but we do it to get a crown that will last for ever. Therefore I do not run like a man running aimlessly; I do not fight like a man beating the air. No, I beat my body and make it my slave so that after I have preached to others, I myself will not be disqualified for the prize.

sportsman and when he lived at home we would often watch the athletics together. I think one of the worst experiences for these great athletes must be to think that you have won the race as you cross the finish line, but later discover that you have been disqualified for breaking a rule. Maybe they had run just outside their track on the bend for a few seconds, but it was enough to get them disqualified and lose their medal. The agony on their faces at such times was terrible! So today consider: what are the "rules" that you sometimes break that you need to discipline? We must

Something to live for...

discipline our bodies, appetites, and actions in order to become consistent winners!

Just as the word "sacrifice" is unpopular today, the word "discipline" is disliked too. Basically, we do not like our comforts being challenged! We like to do things our own way without being corrected. So, we need to recognize these traits in our natural behaviour, but as those called to be champions, those who will pay the price and hit the mark, we need to live differently. The word "disciple" comes from a Latin word meaning "learner", so the word "discipline" comes with this root meaning of being one who is open to instruction and knowledge. In other words, a disciplined person is teachable and open to change. We will be eager to learn

and adapt our life to improve and advance. We will appreciate the advice of a teacher and let them coach our life, correcting errors and making changes to develop our skills. We will alter habits to improve our character, finances, and personality. We will want to strive for the best and let others direct us. After observing great achievers, Harry Truman noted that they had a common quality and said this: "In reading the lives of great men, I found that the first victory they won was over themselves: self-discipline with all of them came first."

In my twenties I had a serious road traffic accident. I needed intensive physiotherapy to learn to walk again. Week after week I was "disciplined" in the physiotherapy department. Most of it was unpleasant and uncomfortable. I was amazed at how quickly I had become attached to my wheelchair and the sense of security it gave to me. When the physiotherapist asked me to get up from my chair, I felt irritated at the way she just grabbed me, moved my chair, and then asked me to walk. Fear overwhelmed me and I felt convinced that I would fall and fail. But under her strict supervision I discovered I could walk – my severely fractured legs had healed and I could balance once more. However, I had to learn to trust her instruction. Many times I wanted to argue, and suggest that the standard was too high or the expectation too great. But again and again I found that if I listened I could walk the distance and make the grade. Today, decide to enrol in the school of training and discover you, too, can make the grade!

HEARTCRY OF PRAYER:

Holy Spirit, today be my mentor and coach and train me for life. I pray that I will know a new level of discipline and obedience. Help me to respond with the right attitudes and make consistent good choices with my life so that I run my race well and quality with excellence. Let me be someone who is not afraid of the challenge of discipline and hard work. Develop in my life a teachable attitude that loves Your ways. Thank You for helping me cross the line as a winner. Amen.

I SURRENDER ALL!

DAY 24

ACTIVATION AND FOCUS:

One of the hardest battles of life is learning to sacrifice our reputation and ambitions. It is so hard to be misunderstood and not to justify our actions. People can often interpret our generosity as interfering or our advice as pressure, and our well-meant actions can be falsely accused. When this happens, it is not always easy to discipline your tongue and let the accusation pass without comment. One of the greatest sacrifices we can give to God is our reputation. Will you be obedient whatever the reaction of your family and friends around you?

Usually somewhere along the path of life God will ask you to do something that will be misunderstood and not help your self-image! Noah was asked to build an ark, miles away from any sea. You may be asked to sacrifice a job without knowing what the future holds, or, like Abraham, told to change where you

 Philippians 2:3–5

Do nothing out of selfish ambition or vain conceit, but in humility consider others better than yourselves. Each of you should look not only to your own interests, but also to the interests of others. Your attitude should be the same as that of Christ Jesus…

 Titus 2:6–8

Similarly, encourage the young men to be self-controlled. In everything set them an example by doing what is good. In your teaching show integrity, seriousness and soundness of speech that cannot be condemned, so that those who oppose you may be ashamed because they have nothing bad to say about us.

live without really knowing where you are going. I remember when God told Gordon to leave the army; it was hard to tell his parents. They had been an army family for years and were proud of their son's achievements. So when he told them he was leaving but had no job yet, this caused confusion and seemed to lack wisdom. To his family Gordon looked irresponsible and foolish but to God he was obedient! Later Gordon's parents understood the decision and respected him greatly, but at the time it was tough.

I remember while living in Malaysia listening to some teaching by Mike Bickle. I was just beginning to speak in public, so the platform experience was very new and I loved it. However, I felt confused by this passion to preach because of my awareness of the need for humility. In his teaching Mike Bickle described two challenges that we need to overcome: the drive to make ourselves "king", and then the time when others want to make us their "king" with all that the popularity game entails. First he explained the need to balance the strength of a call with the self-seeking ambition for reputation and greatness. He taught me to distinguish between the personal desire to make myself "king", the striving that makes you too aware of position and prominence, and the call of God, which has an urgency of its own.

Basically we need to recognize that if the motivation for an activity is God-centred, it will make God look greater, and our commitment to the cause will not diminish even when criticism comes. But if the vision is more self-seeking, when trouble comes, we will compromise our language or change our focus in order

to keep our popularity. If our reputation matters too much, then our activity has become more about us than about God and His name.

However, once you have learnt to handle the battle of your reputation, the next battle is more subtle. How should we react when others want to make us "king"? In other words, how will we respond when people comment and say: "I like your preaching better"; or "I wish you were my friend"; or "I think you are much nicer than my parents". Will we let these compliments boost our pride and elevate our image of ourselves? Even well-meant compliments can be a dangerous seed that stirs illegitimate self-seeking ambitions. We need to deal speedily with these thoughts and temptations, with every ambitious attitude of self-promotion, and not entertain other people's plans to promote us. Let God make your way for you and do not strive!

HEARTCRY OF PRAYER:

Help me to give You a willing sacrifice of my ambitions, dreams, and plans. Help me to do what is right even when I know I could be blamed and misunderstood. Let me fear You more than the loss of my reputation. Teach me Your wisdom to deal with every temptation to make myself "king" or other's pressure to wrongly promote me. Thank You, Father, for this grace. Amen.

DAY 25 — LEAVING AND CLEAVING

ACTIVATION AND FOCUS:

Often we think of the phrase "leaving and cleaving" in association with marriage, but I think it should equally apply to our relationship with Jesus. It is easier to sing songs like "I give you everything" than to live it! Usually the relationships and affections we have are not sinful in and of themselves, but they can become snares if they hold us in a wrong position in our lives. It will always cost you something to give God the highest place. These verses do not say we should not love our family, but just remind us that they should not have the first place in our affections and resulting decisions. When we choose to get married, we understand that we will have to change personal lifestyle choices for the sake of the new partnership, but we are ready to do this because we love deeply; so also we need to be ready to

 Matthew 10:37–39

Anyone who loves his father or mother more than me is not worthy of me; anyone who loves his son or daughter more than me is not worthy of me; and anyone who does not take his cross and follow me is not worthy of me. Whoever finds his life will lose it, and whoever loses his life for my sake will find it.

Mark 10:29–31

"I tell you the truth," Jesus replied, "no one who has left home or brothers or sisters or mother or father or children or fields for me and the gospel will fail to receive a hundred times as much in this present age (homes, brothers, sisters, mothers, children and fields – and with them, persecutions) and in the age to come, eternal life. But many who are first will be last, and the last first."

sacrifice our preferences for the sake of God. We need to release our children to make radical decisions for God and not pressurize them with our desires. My daughter married an Australian, and I knew this would mean my grandchildren would grow up a long way away, but I also knew this marriage was made in heaven so I had to let go of my dreams and release them to go.

I remember when my parents made the decision to send me to boarding school while they remained on the mission field in India. This was not an easy decision for any of us in the family. I did not want to go and my parents did not want to lose me, but for the sake of the call of God to India I needed to go. I have found the promise shown in Mark above to be true: although we paid a price of sacrifice, we have reaped a reward of blessing on this earth too! We had to give up our home and family time but God has blessed us with so much in our later lives.

Again and again if you read the stories of laid-down lives you will notice this thread of sacrifice concerning relationships. Some people have to sacrifice a promise of marriage for the sake of the call. I know a wonderful lady missionary in India who, when younger, sacrificed the love of her life and broke her engagement when she realized that he did not have a call to the mission field and would not leave England or his family. She never met anyone on the field, and served for many years alone. Finally she retired and returned to England, and was apprehensive about living this later period of her life alone in a strange nation. She joined a church, fell in love with a wonderful widower in the congregation, and found that God supplied her with a perfect partner for her old age.

So even if now is the time of sacrifice and readjustment of precious relationships, do not let anxiety tell you that you will lose everything. This is not true. You may sacrifice today, but you will always gain more both in this life and the life to come. So do not fear to let go of those things you know you should not hold so tightly!

HEARTCRY OF PRAYER:

Father, today I give You my affections and family, and I trust You to guide me to do all things well. I yield to You my home, family, and relationships, and ask You to direct my time, choices, and desires for each of them. Help me keep Your plans for my life in the highest place and not manipulate people to do what I want. Please help me not to let my emotional desires rule my life. Let me see in my life and the lives of those around me the promise of blessing where we have sacrificed. Thank You for blessing our homes and lives as we yield them to You afresh. Amen.

DAY 26 NO MORE CLUTTER

ACTIVATION AND FOCUS:

We live in a strange age when what car we drive or what clothes we wear often defines our value more than our character does! As a culture, we have become preoccupied with "things" and overwhelmed by the false need to have more "stuff". The advertising world pressurizes us to buy the latest and greatest technical toy, while every need is pandered to and supplied instantly. We live in a materialistic age where possessions have become obsessions! However, as we watch the consequences of this lifestyle begin to hit our nations with stock markets crashing and banks failing, we need to re-evaluate this way of life. Here, in the first Scripture, the Bible warns us to resist an attitude of greed because it will destroy our life. Watch out, this verse exclaims, you are about to be trapped by an abundance of things, and this

Luke 12:15

Then he said to them, "Watch out! Be on your guard against all kinds of greed; a man's life does not consist in the abundance of his possessions."

Matthew 6:31–33

So do not worry, saying, "What shall we eat?" or "What shall we drink?" or "What shall we wear?" For the pagans run after all these things, and your heavenly Father knows that you need them. But seek first his kingdom and his righteousness, and all these things will be given to you as well.

will ensnare you! We need to deal with every wrong materialistic desire and crucify it, or it will rob our race.

We need to discipline our finances, ask God to supply all our needs, and then live within our means. In society today too many people have sizeable amounts of personal debt but keep spending. These debts then become a trap, weighing people down with worry and even restricting their ability to obey God's call. I met a wonderful couple who knew even from university days that they were called to go to the mission field in North Africa. But, after a series of bad choices, they were left in such terrible debt that they could not, in the natural order of things, pay or work their way out of the debts for about twenty-five years. They realized that their lack of discipline in earlier years could now cost them their dream. This is a hard lesson to learn. I believe that money is not given to us primarily to look after our needs but as a wonderful tool that we should use to care for others around us. We are to be people of generosity and should constantly seek to bless others with our money and gifts. I often say I pray for God to bless my finances so that I can upgrade my standard of giving, not just my standard of living! We need to have money, but learn to use and steward it wisely.

Yet we must not let the fear of having no money control us either. As the economic climate hits families and financial times are tough, we must not worry. This second Scripture promises us that, if we put God first, He will take care of our needs. Recently, I was reading the Lord's Prayer again and stopped to consider

the phrase, "Give us today our daily bread." I realized that God supplies all our needs one day at a time. We want God to guarantee our future financial security, a healthy pension, and adequate savings. God does not necessarily guarantee this request, but does promise He will supply our needs every day. Today God will give you your food, money for the bills, and clothes to wear. Today God will take care of your financial needs, so do not worry. So often in my life, when I have thought I have stretched too far, believed for too much, God has supplied the salary, the food, the money for the fuel to travel. God has never failed but He has kept me panicking to the last minute sometimes! So do not let your mind get cluttered with fears about money – today decide to trust and watch for God's supply.

HEARTCRY OF PRAYER:

Father, teach me to be more disciplined in the area of my finances. Help me discern between greedy desires and legitimate needs. Teach me to be more disciplined with my money and use it wisely. Show me when to be generous and bless others. Help me know that as I sacrifice and seek Your will first, You will take care of my needs. Let me seek Your kingdom more than my own desires. Thank You for breaking the fear of money in my life and letting me live free. Amen.

DAY 27 — WHAT CAN I GIVE?

It is the fragrant sacrifice of seemingly small choices that delights the heart of God. As we choose to live a life of discipline and sacrifice, we often find it is the ordinary, daily discipline of consistently doing the right thing that pleases God and impacts others deeply. Each day we need to have this attitude: what can I improve today, or how can I live with a greater authenticity? In our everyday routines we need to constantly submit our decisions to God and ask Him to help us choose the right thing. If we want to live a disciplined life, we need to learn when to switch the TV off and do something different. We

Ephesians 5:1–3

Be imitators of God, therefore, as dearly loved children and live a life of love, just as Christ loved us and gave himself up for us as a fragrant offering and sacrifice to God. But among you there must not be even a hint of sexual immorality, or of any kind of impurity, or of greed, because these are improper for God's holy people.

Hebrews 13:15–16

Through Jesus, therefore, let us continually offer to God a sacrifice of praise – the fruit of lips that confess his name. And do not forget to do good and to share with others, for with such sacrifices God is pleased.

need to be sensitive about what we read and eat, and be ready to change our lifestyle habits to improve our discipline. We need to

... something worth dying for!

be a people who are flexible and ready to give up our rights for a better reward. If we really take up the challenge of daily sacrifice it will change everything!

I remember when I was leading a ladies Bible study group, I commented on some of the popular women's magazines and trendy reading material. I questioned if it was helpful for the greater race of life to fill our minds with so much sex, scandal, and stories of "friendly" vampires. Fortunately, the members of my group knew that I am not boring and I love to have fun – but we do need to discipline our sources of entertainment. Are we choosing the right triggers to help us have a laugh? Often we feel awkward when talking in such detail about these basic life decisions, as we do not want to appear old fashioned or legalistic. But we do need to have the courage to seriously examine these everyday leisure activities and evaluate whether they are the best diet to help us relax.

The Bible talks about the different levels of harvest we can reap with our lives. In the Parable of the Sower it points out that if we take the word of God and invest it in our hearts we can see a 30 per cent, 60 per cent, or 100 per cent harvest depending on the condition of our heart, the level of our obedience, and the persistence of our faith. The choice is ours! We will reap a harvest – but the quality and quantity will be determined by our decisions.

One of the hardest disciplines I have had to learn is how to spend my time. I love meeting with friends and having time to walk

and talk, but it takes time. When I began to minister, was trying to run a busy house with two teenagers, and was supporting Gordon while he pastored a big church, I found time was stretched. I would try to have my friendship time, but this was at the cost of preparation time for my next ministry engagement. One day I was praying as once again I had little time to prepare, and I felt God ask me if I would sacrifice my friendship time for the ministry He was calling me to have. I struggled, as this was my relaxation time and I did not want to let it go, but I knew I had a choice. Soon after this time with God I was at a meeting and Cindy Jacobs

... something worth dying for!

prophesied that I should begin to write, and again I wondered where I would find the time. Again God challenged me to give up some of my leisure time and write. It has not always been easy but I know it has been right, and I have found that the friendship time I do have has been multiplied in quality even though the quantity has been reduced! So, read the Scriptures above one more time and then pray!

HEARTCRY OF PRAYER:

Father, help me make the everyday choices that will keep my life on track. Help me use my time and plan my schedules wisely so that I honour Your call upon my life. I ask You, Lord, to show me what adjustments I need to make so that my life blesses You more. Let the choices that I make cause my life to be more attractive to people around me. Father, keep me from every compromising decision and let me show Your heart to others. Thank You, Father. Amen.

DAY 28 THE WINNING TEAM

ACTIVATION AND FOCUS:

In these Scriptures we are encouraged to recognize discipline as the friend who will enable us to run our race like a champion. We have a stadium of heroes who have completed their race, and who are now cheering us forward, reminding us to run with perseverance and not give up. We are part of an eternal relay race and we have the best coach who will train us for excellence.

George Washington left us with a wonderful

⌃ Hebrews 12:1–3

Therefore, since we are surrounded by such a great cloud of witnesses, let us throw off everything that hinders and the sin that so easily entangles, and let us run with perseverance the race marked out for us. Let us fix our eyes on Jesus, the author and perfecter of our faith, who for the joy set before him endured the cross, scorning its shame, and sat down at the right hand of the throne of God. Consider him who endured such opposition from sinful men, so that you will not grow weary and lose heart.

⌃ Hebrews 12: 5–7, 11

And you have forgotten that word of encouragement that addresses you as sons:
"My son, do not make light of the Lord's discipline, and do not lose heart when he rebukes you, because the Lord disciplines those he loves, and he punishes everyone he accepts as a son."

Endure hardship as discipline; God is treating you as sons… No discipline seems pleasant at the time, but painful. Later on, however, it produces a harvest of righteousness and peace for those who have been trained by it.

Something to live for...

challenge in this quote: "Discipline is the soul of an army. It makes small numbers formidable; procures success to the weak, and esteem to all." It is so easy to get absorbed with personal success and forget the bigger picture of working together as a team. We must cross the line together and enjoy each of us being a winner as we run our race.

I remember chatting to my husband, Gordon, about his officer training in the army. He recalled that one of the lessons he had to learn quickly was how to work as a team and ensure that everyone was working in their area of gifting, fulfilling their potential. Many of their training exercises involved taking responsibility for those around you and helping them complete the tasks within the expected time, not just getting the best time for yourself. You were only finished when the whole team crossed the line. You could not rely on your personal achievement alone to promote you, you had to learn to watch for others and help them succeed too if you wanted to pass your exams and become an officer.

I believe that this insight addresses so much of the competitiveness that we see in the church. We should play to our strengths and be ready to cover our friends' weaknesses. We should be watching and helping each other reflect Christ more completely in our neighbourhoods and nations. This is the time for us to stand together as a disciplined army, ready to sacrifice for the greater good. The race we are called to run is not just about us and our personal success, but depends totally upon us having the right response and making good decisions. A good leader is one who can motivate his troops to volunteer and sacrifice their lives because of their respect for him and their commitment to the cause. So let us run this race with excellence ensuring that we all win the prize! Before you pray, take a moment to consider the challenges you have felt as you have read this week's meditations. Then make the choice to change.

HEARTCRY OF PRAYER:

Father, give me a new awareness of those around me. Help me run my race with a passion to see others succeed. Deliver me from all competitiveness and jealousy that could limit my race. As I read these Scriptures again, help me to recognize Your instruction in my life and help me to be trained by it. Let me embrace difficulty, understanding that there can be a harvest of blessing if I respond correctly. Let me hear those crowds of witnesses encouraging me to run. Amen.

WEEK FIVE:

DANGEROUS
PASSION

DANGEROUS

Causing danger; perilous;
circumstances that are able or likely to cause injury or harm;
hazardous, jeopardizing, risky, serious, **threatening**, unsafe,
venturesome;
adventure that requires risk.

PASSION

Strong and barely controllable emotion;
intense, driving, or overwhelming feeling;
strong conviction, deep affection, barely containable love;
a strong desire or devotion to a certain activity, object, or concept;
used to describe the **sufferings of Christ** between the night of
the Last Supper and His death.

> **As soon as there is life there is danger.**
> RALPH WALDO EMERSON

> **Nothing great in the world has ever been accomplished without passion.**
>
> HEGEL

> **The most dangerous thing in the world is to try to leap a chasm in two jumps.**
>
> DAVID LLOYD GEORGE

SOMETHING TO LIVE FOR...

... SOMETHING WORTH DYING FOR!

DAY 29 A LIFE OF CONVICTION

ACTIVATION AND FOCUS:

I do not know if you can remember the first time the power of the words of Jesus gripped your life. I can remember sitting in a cow shed in the north of England during the Dales Bible Week. I was seventeen years old and the preacher was speaking about the kingdom of God. As I listened to his message, everything within me decided that I would dedicate my life to carrying this message of Jesus. I was utterly convinced this was how I wanted to spend the rest of my life: passionately given to carry the good news of Jesus who can heal, deliver, save, and transform. I was called and captivated that night by the power of the Gospel.

> **1 Thessalonians 1:4–5**
> For we know, brothers loved by God, that he has chosen you, because our gospel came to you not simply with words, but also with power, with the Holy Spirit and with deep conviction.

> **Romans 8:38–39**
> For I am convinced that neither death nor life, neither angels nor demons, neither the present nor the future, nor any powers, neither height nor depth, nor anything else in all creation, will be able to separate us from the love of God that is in Christ Jesus our Lord.

Can you remember those times of encounter with God? Those moments of deep conviction, when you knew you were called to live a dangerous life as a passionate lover of God?

Che Guevara expresses dangerous passion as follows: "We cannot be sure of having something to live for unless we are

willing to die for it." We should be totally convinced about Jesus and His way of living. There should be a dangerous inflexibility that will not compromise the truth or lower our standards. We should believe that Jesus is the only way and not bend to be acceptably inclusive of other religions or lifestyles. Although an unpopular stand in today's tolerant culture, we should be prepared to be known as fanatics, outrageous carriers of the love of God.

The Church should be an extreme gathering of people who are absolutely persuaded that the love of God is real. We are called to infect our communities with the revelation of this incredible love that can change everything. God's love does not ask us to be tolerant and accepting of people's compromise, but to be compassionate and strategic in helping these people get free. If you were to see someone drowning in a lake and crying for help, would you throw them a sleeping pill and say, "Take this pill, it will help you forget the pain as you die", or would you find a life raft, throw it to them and rescue them from the cold water? Political correctness is like giving a drowning person a sleeping pill and saying "Die in peace", but not wanting to interfere in their choice of life even though you can see they are dying. We need to be utterly convinced that the love of God never fails. We are not called to apologize but to evangelize!

So what is the fuel of this intense fire? An absolute conviction that God's love never fails. Once you know, that you know, that you know God loves you, it changes everything! You will carry this message and watch people get free. God's love is like the warm breeze that melts the frozen landscape, turning the dull, grey scenery into full, vibrant colour. Touch someone with this message of love and watch the transformation!

HEARTCRY OF PRAYER:

Father, remind me of those moments of encounter when I knew I was challenged to live a dedicated life. I am sorry for the times that I have hesitated in sharing my faith with others. Release me from any tolerance that extinguishes my passion. Refresh my knowledge of the love of God. Let me be an infectious carrier of this love to many around me. Help me carry an absolute knowledge that Your love NEVER fails. Amen.

Something to live for...

RISKY LIVING

ACTIVATION AND FOCUS:

In this Scripture we are reminded that the Christian life is a life full of adventure. We are called to take risks that will not make sense to the casual observer. God gives us promises, but we have to step out into the unknown and watch them unfold. This takes courage and perseverance. Usually the path feels dangerous and insecure, but we have to lean into the goodness of God and trust Him to do what He has promised He will. These challenges of faith are never convenient or easy but, once completed, they are satisfying and fulfilling. However, to walk this dangerous journey of faith we must deepen our trust.

 Romans 4:18–21

Against all hope, Abraham in hope believed and so became the father of many nations, just as it had been said to him, "So shall your offspring be." Without weakening in his faith, he faced the fact that his body was as good as dead – since he was about a hundred years old – and that Sarah's womb was also dead. Yet he did not waver through unbelief regarding the promise of God, but was strengthened in his faith and gave glory to God, being fully persuaded that God had power to do what he had promised.

Most of us are cautious and do not like to live our life on a knife-edge, feeling that at any moment everything could go over the abyss. But there are seasons when God challenges us to let go of all our securities and let Him direct us. I remember when we returned to England and were about to buy our house. We

had no money or credit rating with which to obtain a mortgage because we had been missionaries in Africa for the previous six years. But we knew God had spoken to us about buying my parents' home, as they were moving to the States. It seemed impossible. People gave generously to us at this time, but we still could not get the maths to work by the completion date. We were a considerable amount of money short. We prayed and fasted and, to be honest, panicked a little. Just two days before the completion date a building society phoned us and said that they had reconsidered our case, changed their mind, and were willing to give us a loan. This perfectly provided for the shortfall. For weeks we had walked on water but at the last minute God made a way for us. Alfred Adler challenges us with this thought: "The chief danger in life is that you may take too many precautions." So step out and remember faith is often spelt R-I-S-K!

When we walk this path of faith we must learn to face the facts but believe the truth. Often I meet people who are frightened to face the facts of their circumstances, as they have an almost

Something to live for...

superstitious mindset that fears that if they admit how bad things are they might jeopardize their faith, and so disqualify themselves from God's help. Like Abraham we need to face the facts but still be determined that, although the circumstances look bad, God has the power to do what he has promised. I have met people who will not look at their bank statements or read their doctor's reports for fear of facing the facts. We need to identify the problem, but then be able to see a BIG God who is more than able to help us. In Portugal I remember watching the face of a man who had been tested HIV positive return to the doctor, undergo another test after prayer, and then return with a new certificate declaring him HIV negative. The power of seeing this man stand with both certificates and celebrate the healing power of Jesus was overwhelming.

HEARTCRY OF PRAYER:

Father, today I commit myself to a life engaged in faith adventures. Teach me to hear Your word and then trust You to fulfil it. Please keep me from all doubt and uncertainty that robs my confidence to respond to Your promises. Help me develop my trust in Your goodness. Heal me where I have been disappointed by the lack of answers to my prayers or the long periods of delay. Restore in me the desire to live my life on the cutting edge of faith and help me take hold of my promises. Amen.

DAY 31 ZEAL FOR HIS HOUSE

ACTIVATION AND FOCUS:

Even the quietest person can be triggered into a strong campaigner if you touch on a subject they are passionate about. Gordon and I were house group leaders for many years and we enjoyed our large but diverse group that met in our home each Wednesday. There was one girl in our group who seemed shy and was reticent in group discussions until the night of Monopoly. Suddenly we found her passion to win! That night a transformation took place and our shy, reticent girl held forth, bargained for the cards, shouted at the bank, and won the game! I wonder, what triggers your passion?

I love church! I know this statement immediately causes a reaction because many of us have had negative experiences in church, but we must overcome these memories and be passionate

> **2 Kings 19:30–31**
>
> Once more a remnant of the house of Judah will take root below and bear fruit above. For out of Jerusalem will come a remnant, and out of Mount Zion a band of survivors. The zeal of the LORD Almighty will accomplish this.

> **John 2:16–17**
>
> To those who sold doves he said, "Get these out of here! How dare you turn my Father's house into a market!" His disciples remembered that it is written: "Zeal for your house will consume me."

about church. In these two Scriptures we see that God has a zealous passion for His house and that He is looking for a band of people who will work with Him. I really believe that good church is the answer for the needs of our society. I agree that so much that is called "church" does not represent God's original design, so we need to get back to the Bible and build a great house that looks like God's home. I believe that a backslidden nation is a reflection of a sleeping church. We need to arise with a passionate call and build good church. Here Jesus rebukes the religious leaders of the time for changing the priorities of the Temple to make it a place of commercial venture rather than a house of worship and prayer. Church needs to be more about people than our projects. It should be a house of welcome to the hurting of our neighbourhood where they can find love, hope, and acceptance. It is time for the church to be turned inside out. We need to arise and take the love of God out onto the streets.

Why do I believe in church? We are called to be the bride of Christ. I have attended many weddings in my life, but the beauty of a bride walking with great love and expectation down the aisle towards her bridegroom never ceases to amaze me. So this bride, the church, should take her opportunity to walk down the aisle of our neighbourhoods, looking fantastic, so that

people get a glimpse of our passionate love for God. It is easy to grow so familiar with the concept of "church" and then lose the vision of its gift to society. Do not grow familiar with precious things but today ask God to stir a new affection for His church. Church should not be centred on serving our personal preferences, but rather focused on answering the needs of the broken. Church

Something to live for...

should not be about us but for them! Let God give you His zeal for His house, and let a new vision consume you. I long to see thousands of passionate churches built across our nations, standing like beacons of hope for people in their time of trouble and distress. Let us arise and build good church.

HEARTCRY OF PRAYER:

Father, I ask You to forgive me where I have had a negative attitude towards Your house. Give me a fresh revelation and love for Your church. Show me how I can become a part of the fruitful remnant who build Your church in these days. Father, let Your church arise in the nation and be a sign of Your love and goodness. Forgive us for not speaking Your name with passion. Amen.

DAY 32 A POWERFUL PARTNERSHIP

ACTIVATION AND FOCUS:

A healthy partnership between zeal and wisdom is essential if we are to achieve our goals. All through Scripture we can observe this balance of zeal, passion, power, and big vision being tempered by the boundaries, principles, reality, and order of wise counsel. Benjamin Franklin describes this partnership as follows: "If passion drives you, then let reason hold the reins." We all have seasons in our lives when we know we are high on zeal but lower on wisdom, or vice versa. Usually when we are young we are motivated by great passion but still learning wisdom. As we get older we can tend to have matured in wisdom but lost our zeal. This can result in a generational tension: the young feel constrained by the constant limitations placed on their adventurous plans, and the older people feel their wisdom is ignored.

If we do not understand the power of this partnership then,

> **Proverbs 19:2**
> It is not good to have zeal without knowledge, nor to be hasty and miss the way.
>
> **Romans 10:2**
> For I can testify about them that they are zealous for God, but their zeal is not based on knowledge.
>
> **Romans 12:11**
> Never be lacking in zeal, but keep your spiritual fervour, serving the Lord.

to the zealous, wisdom can look like the attitude that spoils the party, limits our passion, and just brings a legalistic control or irritating caution. But equally, to the mature, zeal can look like blatant irresponsibility, arrogance accompanied by big ideas with no substance, or stupidity that will cause heartache and produce nothing. Often these characteristics of passion and wisdom can cause conflict, but we must learn to bring them into partnership if we are to have great success!

Emerson notes that "Passion, though a bad regulator, is a powerful spring." There are twenty-one references to the zeal of the Lord in the Bible, and we are commanded in Romans to never be lacking in zeal. Yet most of us find there is a trade-off between wisdom and zeal as we get older – we lose passion but gain some understanding. We consider this acceptable, dismissing our loss of vision with comments such as, "Well, I am older and wiser now." However, I do not believe that God ever wants us to lose the passion of our call. Once again let us remind ourselves of this Scripture in Romans 12:11, "Never be lacking in zeal, but keep your spiritual fervour, serving the Lord."

Yet as our passion grows, let us keep our ears open for the advice of wisdom. We can be passionate, but passionately wrong, and one word of experience can help us succeed. I remember an occasion when I got into my car excited: we were driving to Kisumu, Kenya, to be with Reinhard Bonnke for some meetings. I was convinced I knew the way and, even when road signs began to contradict my planned route, I was certain I was right.

My excitement clouded my judgment. After several hours I was confused, for we should have arrived long since, but Kisumu was nowhere to be seen. Others in the car had suggested we stop and ask for directions, but I had insisted I knew the way. I did not want to stop and waste time: I just wanted to drive. Finally we stopped, lost and tired, and discovered we had taken a wrong turn onto a new road. My excitement to drive and my decision to ignore the advice of others had cost us six hours! A lesson well learnt; do not be too proud to ask for advice.

HEARTCRY OF PRAYER:

Father, reveal to me where I need to stir passion and cherish wisdom more. Forgive me for the times when I have quenched someone's zeal with my cynicism or ignored advice due to my pride. Help me learn to recognize this partnership of zeal and wisdom and apply it to my life. Let me encourage the passionate and advise the unsure with wisdom. Thank You, Father. Amen.

DAY 33 — PASSIONATE PURSUITS

ACTIVATION AND FOCUS:

As we read these Scriptures we should realize that God is passionate about our success. God does not want us to remain mediocre or average, but rather to excel and be significant. We can have a false understanding of humility, believing that we should remain insignificant and unknown. But if we are connected to a great God we should find that our passionate pursuit of Him causes us to become partners in His greatness. In these verses God speaks about our character and legacy of excellence. As expressed in this quote by Ingersoll, "In the world of mediocrity, genius is dangerous", the church is often more comfortable with a theology of lowliness and limited profile, but God wants to give us a legacy of greatness that lasts for generations.

> **Psalm 45:2**
> You are the most excellent of men and your lips have been anointed with grace, since God has blessed you for ever.
>
> **Psalm 45:16–17**
> Your sons will take the place of your fathers; you will make them princes throughout the land. I will perpetuate your memory through all generations; therefore the nations will praise you for ever and ever.
>
> **1 Timothy 3:13**
> Those who have served well gain an excellent standing and great assurance in their faith in Christ Jesus.

We are called to be extravagant lovers of God who are ready to work for the King. We need to know that because of our relationship

with Jesus, we carry the supernatural DNA of heaven. Although we were born ordinary, God does not want us to live ordinary lives. On 29 April 2011 Prince William married Kate Middleton. As I watched the moment the future King of England married his beautiful bride, the Holy Spirit spoke to me about the privilege of being part of a kingdom. I noticed that the American media was distressed that the British press called Kate a "commoner", but I realized that we understand "kingdom" language in the UK, and that by calling Kate a commoner we simply acknowledged the fact that she had no royal blood.

In the same way, all of us are commoners or sinners before we surrender our lives to Jesus. And yet, we have turned the head of the King of Kings and He counts us worthy to be His bride. Just as Kate Middleton's marriage covenant with Prince William changed her status, name, and authority, so our covenant commitment to the King of Heaven changes everything. Through this covenant we gain kingdom authority and become co-heirs with Christ. When Kate walked into Westminster Abbey no one saluted her, but on her exit with the future king everyone acknowledged her – she was no longer a commoner. Kate now has authority in the British royal household and so do we, in God's kingdom, once we are joined to Christ. Although a commoner by birth, it is now impossible for Kate to give birth to a commoner: she will only give birth to royal princes and princesses. In the same way, we now carry the King's word and so are called to "make princes in the land". We no longer carry the ordinary but the extraordinary, no longer just the natural but the supernatural!

So reflect on the richness of this imagery from the royal wedding and let God fill you with a deeper sense of wonder for what He has given to us as His Bride. It is time for the church to carry her dignity and walk like the bride of the King. It is time to raise princes in the land who will lead with courage. We need to mentor the next generation into their roles of influence. We have a royal commission from heaven and we cannot remain silent, so let us stand up boldly and passionately pursue excellence for our nations and the next generation.

HEARTCRY OF PRAYER:

Father, thank You that You have called us to an excellent way. You have placed within us a desire to be the best and to win the prize. Father, confront in my life every attitude of false humility that robs me of my dignity. Raise us to be people of influence and significance in our nation. Let us be the head and not the tail. Advance our leadership in society so that we can be a voice of help in times of trouble. Father, I thank You that You have passionately pursued me as Your bride. Amen.

FOR THIS CAUSE!

ACTIVATION AND FOCUS:

When life becomes dangerous we must remember our mission. Like Jesus, we need to remember the reason for our being on earth, and make the choice to stand and fulfil our purpose. Both Jesus and Esther were confronted with a moment of decision in a time of crisis and knew it was their time to press through. Both Esther and Jesus had to consider the possibility of death and decide they were ready to give their life. Jesus died and won; Esther faced death, lived and triumphed. John Maxwell underlines for us this necessary partnership between passion and courage: "A great leader's courage to fulfil his vision comes from passion, not position." If we are passionate about the cause we will have courage to see it through! A title or position will not help us in that moment, but our conviction and faith will.

William Hunter, born 1535 in Brentwood, Essex, was apprenticed

 John 12:27–28

Now my heart is troubled, and what shall I say? "Father, save me from this hour"? No, it was for this very reason I came to this hour. Father, glorify your name!

 Esther 4:13–14

"Do not think that because you are in the king's house you alone of all the Jews will escape. For if you remain silent at this time, relief and deliverance for the Jews will arise from another place, but you and your father's family will perish. And who knows but that you have come to royal position for such a time as this?"

to a silk weaver in London. There he discovered the Bible, began to read it in English for himself and became passionate about it. He then refused to attend mass, going against an order that everyone in the City of London had to attend the Catholic mass. By refusing to obey, William lost his job and so returned to Brentwood. There, it soon became apparent that William held Protestant beliefs and refused to deny his faith in Jesus. He was imprisoned for nine months, but continued to refuse to renounce his beliefs, even in the face of threats, physical punishment, and bribery. Eventually William was sentenced to death and executed for being found reading the Bible in English. He was publicly burned at the age of nineteen. It would seem that the authorities were particularly incensed by the spiritual maturity and passion for God in someone so young. William found a cause and he was ready to die rather than deny it. All through history we read the stories of incredible people who stand and die rather than deny God. They have found something to live for and something worth dying for!

Not all of us will be asked to die for our cause, but all of us will be required to make sacrifices and adjustments. This passionate love for God is a dangerous business. Are you ready to embrace a dangerous passion and yield your life to God 100 per cent? I remember driving on a road in Zambia and being stopped by armed bandits with guns who threatened to kill me. We had only just arrived in Africa to serve as missionaries, and I was confronted with guns and the challenge of whether I was ready to die. I remember thinking in that second: "Well, I am in a WIN-WIN

Statues of twentieth century Christian martyrs, Westminster Abbey.

situation. If I die I go to heaven and see Jesus and if I live I can work in Africa. So live or die – I win!"

HEARTCRY OF PRAYER:

Father, today I give my life to the greater cause of Your kingdom. Help me live for You without compromise or fear. Help me discern the specific callings You have given to me. Help me to identify those projects and dreams that You have called me to birth and to devote my life and resources to them. Teach me to stand in times of trouble and not renounce Your call on my life. Like Jesus, let me give my life to You afresh and let Your name be glorified through me. Teach me to passionately love Your name above all other things. Amen.

... something worth dying for! 145

WEEK SIX:

DESTINED AS
CHAMPIONS

DESTINED

decreed beforehand, predetermined;
designated, assigned, or dedicated in advance;
directed, devised, or set apart for a specific purpose or place.

CHAMPION

a warrior, a fighter;
militant advocate or defender of civil rights;
one that does battle for another's rights or honour;
a winner of first prize or first place in a competition;
one who shows **marked superiority**.

God will raise me up a champion.
SIR WALTER SCOTT

 The only person you are destined to become is the person you decide to be.

RALPH WALDO EMERSON

Challenge and opportunity are motivating friends of a consistent winner.

ANONYMOUS

SOMETHING TO LIVE FOR...
... SOMETHING WORTH DYING FOR!

Something to live for...

D AY 3 5   BORN TO WIN

ACTIVATION AND FOCUS:

A champion is the combination of extraordinary talent and dedicated hard work. Champions do not just "happen"; they dream, work, struggle, fail, achieve, and then finally win consistently! Every Olympic gold medallist will have lost a

> **1 Corinthians 9:24**
>
> Do you not know that in a race all the runners run, but only one gets the prize? Run in such a way as to get the prize.

significant race they should have won, but they had to get up, train more, and run again. Ziglar reminds us, "You were born to win, but to be a winner, you must plan to win, prepare to win, and expect to win."

So, as you decide to run your race, do not expect to be treated like a champion, cheered, and respected by colleagues, but train like one and then watch and wait as your life will be honoured. The champions we honour now usually started life with difficulties and setbacks, but they knew they were born to overcome. Today we consider them heroes, but when they started out they were often misunderstood, considered strange fanatics, and excluded before they were welcomed and admired. Consider the life of Helen Keller.

Helen Keller was born in Alabama, America, on 27 June 1880. When she was nineteen months old, she suffered from meningitis and became blind and deaf as a result. However, Helen Keller was determined to conquer her setback and excel. She worked hard, overcame her disabilities, and so became the first blind–deaf person to effectively communicate with a world in which vision and sound are so important. Her teacher, Anne Sullivan, played a vital role in this achievement. Helen graduated from college in 1904 (an achievement in itself!) and dedicated her life to helping people with these disabilities. Her dedication, courage, and determination, which were based on her Christian faith, were recognized by many people. Winston Churchill called her "the greatest woman of our age".

I am sure that when people looked at Helen Keller in her childhood years, they did not see a champion. They probably pitied this poor child who was obviously physically challenged. But Helen and her teacher saw something different, and today she is one of the few women with her statue on Capitol Hill. As congressmen and senators unveiled the bronze statue of Helen Keller at the US Capitol, lawmakers praised her as a trailblazer and an inspiration for those with disabilities. In his speech the Governor of Alabama, Bob Riley, said:

It is a defining moment that we celebrate today. This moment is so vividly depicted by this statue of Helen Keller, who helped the world to understand that all of us, regardless of any disability, have a mind that can be educated, a hand that can be trained, a life that will have meaning.

Something to live for...

So, today, know that you were born to win. Whatever the hindrances you see in your life, treat them as friends that will advance your resolve rather than enemies that impede your progress. As we read our Bibles, we see that every hero encountered a trial before they obtained their prize of faith. Either they had failed, were persecuted and mocked, or came from a poor background and were not expected to succeed. Naturally they had nothing to commend them, but they considered God rather than themselves, ran their race with obedience, and won. So run your race: you were born to WIN!

HEARTCRY OF PRAYER:

Today, as I read the stories of other heroes who have fought the fight of faith and won, help me to live life with a new determination to overcome every obstacle. Teach me to regard everyone as a champion, someone born to win, whether they look like one or not. Father, thank You that You take broken, despised, and overlooked people and train them to win. Take my life and every area of weakness and teach me Your attitude. Thank You for the heroes of faith that inspire us by their lives. Let me now run to get my prize! Amen.

DAY 36

DESTINED FOR GREATNESS

"I always knew I was destined for greatness," said Oprah Winfrey in an interview. This may seem exceptionally bold but it is the truth for her and for us. Did you know that God has destined you for greatness? We may have different definitions of what "greatness" looks like, but God made your life to be significant. In this Scripture we read of how God spoke to Abraham and wanted him to understand that he was born to have great influence, and that through him and his children the world would be blessed. Abraham was an impotent, old man at this time and I am sure he did not "feel" special. But God called him GREAT!

 **Genesis 12:2–3**

"I will make you into a great nation and I will bless you; I will make your name great, and you will be a blessing. I will bless those who bless you, and whoever curses you I will curse; and all peoples on earth will be blessed through you."

To many, the church does not look like a credible answer to all the overwhelming social needs in our neighbourhoods, but God has destined us for greatness. Through our lives together we can bring change and hope. Remember that David was overlooked but became an outstanding king, led the nation, and was a hero for the people. The journey to greatness does not usually start in a promising place, as Riley describes for us: "From nobody to upstart. From upstart to contender. From contender to winner. From winner to champion. From champion to Dynasty." This is the path of many who discover they can win, like Eric Liddell.

Eric Liddell was born to missionary parents who served in northern China, and his early years were spent in a London Missionary Society compound. Eric excelled at athletics and rugby, but an event that took place in 1921 changed the direction of his life. Eric was invited to speak about his Christian faith at a public meeting. This was reported in the Scottish press and Eric started to receive many invitations to share the Gospel. He also continued running and was getting faster and faster. He qualified for the 1924 Paris Olympics and gained notoriety when he refused to run in three events because they had been scheduled to be run on a Sunday. Harold Abrahams won gold in the 100 metres, the race that Eric had refused to run in. Eric won bronze in the 200 metres, a race in which he was not expected to do well. He also competed in the 400 metres where there was even less chance, or so the experts thought! Eric not only won the race but set a new world record. Eric had gone from being a Scottish hero, to a coward and traitor, and back to a national hero. Within eighteen months of the Olympics, Eric Liddell had given up athletics and was on his way to China, at a time when the country was in turmoil and the communists were fighting for power. Eric Liddell gave up a life of fame in this world to serve God in China during a time of war and great difficulty. He was a hero to Scotland because he could run fast, but a friend to the Chinese as he shared Jesus. Eric balanced both his natural and spiritual gifts and achieved greatness in both.

Greatness is going to look different to each one of us. Most of us will never stand on podiums receiving gold medals of honour, but instead our greatness will be written on the hearts of men and women who were touched by our lives. Whether in the glare of the media or in a slum in the third world, you were destined for greatness and your life should leave a blessing behind you. Let your life of generosity, action, wisdom, and compassion leave a trail of goodness that will honour you with greatness.

HEARTCRY OF PRAYER:

Father, thank You for all those who have run their race with courage and conviction, and left a legacy of greatness. Father, show me where You want me to give my life and for whom. I thank You for those who have poured out their lives for the broken, but still excelled in their everyday responsibilities too. Teach me to hold my natural and spiritual callings in balance. Amen.

DAY 37 ONE SMALL STEP FOR MAN

ACTIVATION AND FOCUS:

"One small step for man, a giant leap for mankind." So said Neil Armstrong as he walked on the moon. I wonder if he ever realized how famous that statement would become. But the path of champions is usually comprised of many determined, small steps that, in time, gain their significance. It is only history that turns those moments of dogged determination into glory. Champions are usually people who do not know when to give up! Here we

 Genesis 32:28

Then the man said, "Your name will no longer be Jacob, but Israel, because you have struggled with God and with men and have overcome."

 Joshua 1:3

I will give you every place where you set your foot, as I promised Moses.

read about Jacob, an ambitious young man who knew what he wanted. He wrestled and struggled against all the odds but knew what he needed to do. He often did things the hard way but learnt from his mistakes. Adler makes this comment about champions, "Champions know there are no shortcuts to the top. They climb the mountain one step at a time. They have no use for helicopters!" Jacob was one of those!

As you decide to run your race you must realize that you will take your ground one step at a time. God promised Joshua that he would give him every piece of ground, if he first set his foot on

it. We have to go and take our territory. It will require the hard, repetitive task of walking the streets, speaking to people, making connections and developing the strategy. Although God promises us success, we do have to work in our communities and build the relationships before we see the stories of lives transformed. I have loved watching the work of the Message Trust in Manchester as they have built community relationships by living in the deprived city estates (Eden Projects), ministered in schools, worked in the prisons, and poured out their lives for their city. Now they are seeing the results after 25 years of hard labour. How did they find success? Just one step at a time.

Read with me another inspiring story, this time in Egypt, where a businessman stepped into a garbage village and brought change. In the early 1980s this man gave up his job in the city to become an ordained priest in order to minister in this village. When he began, the village had no churches, schools, electricity, water, medical care, or markets. It was just piles of rubbish and people living with pigs in extreme poverty with no sanitation, hope, or care. As Father Samaan took care of the dying and ministered to their needs, thousands met Jesus as their Saviour and then wanted to build Him a house. Thus began a project to build a church in the midst of this poor community.

Today, the garbage village has been transformed and is almost unrecognizable: order has been restored and the crime rate has dropped. The dedicated love of a man who showed them Jesus has changed their lives. The village is now a bustling, hopeful community of 30,000 people. They still collect garbage; however, they have three schools, a hospital, and many churches. The churches they have built are located in caves that were blocked by rubble. While the first cave was being converted into a chapel, residents found another that is now used for healing services of up to 4,000 people. They then discovered yet another cave that was transformed into an enormous amphitheatre to seat 15,000 people. Weekly church meetings gather people from across Cairo, not just the residents of the garbage village. Father Samaan now pastors the largest church in the Middle East and one of the best known in Egypt: St Simon the Tanner Coptic Orthodox Church in the Mokattam garbage village.

So, let us arise and believe that small steps of obedience can influence history. We must not despise "the day of small beginnings", but step out boldly and watch the results in our communities and nations.

HEARTCRY OF PRAYER:

Father, today give me courage to take the small steps of obedience, realizing that they are vital even though they appear insignificant. Let me see beyond the slow progress and resist discouragement, knowing that this obedience will bring success. Let me not despise the day of small beginnings but have the tenacity to walk into my promises step by step. Let me be a champion among the poor, helping them to find life! Amen.

DAY 38   AGAINST THE ODDS

ACTIVATION AND FOCUS:

"A quitter never wins, and a winner never quits." The time just before the finishing line comes into view is the hardest point of a long race. The monotony of the race and the pain in your body scream "it is time to stop", and it is so hard to keep your perspective and realize you are winning the race by persevering just one step at a time. Like a marathon race, the tedious routine of life can feel futile and the temptation to give up or choose a different path is huge. But do not give up!

> **Hebrews 10:38–39**
>
> "But my righteous one will live by faith. And if he shrinks back, I will not be pleased with him." But we are not of those who shrink back and are destroyed, but of those who believe and are saved.

I was counselling a young woman who had young children and whose husband worked long hours, and she was exhausted. "I just want to change my life," she exclaimed. "I want to walk out on my marriage, find a new life, and be happy. I am so tired and so bored. There must be more than this!" We can all sympathize with her frustration, but her conclusion is wrong! We can all identify with those days when we just want to check out of life and do something different, but we must not quit. Success comes to those who wait, persevere, and are patient. This girl worked through her dissatisfaction and today is still married, a great mum with outstanding children. She just kept doing the boring laps of house chores until one day she realized this season of life was completed — now she could have fun and reap the reward of the hard years of mothering. Good mums are some of the best champions never crowned!

Often we think that to have a great finish we need a promising start. But look at these men: Shakepeare's father was a wool merchant; the Emperor Diocletian was the son of a slave; Abraham Lincoln's father was a poor farmer and labourer; Cardinal Antonelli's father was an Italian bandit; the father of Adrian, the ascetic pontiff, was a beggar; Virgil's father was a porter and for years a slave; Ben Franklin was the son of a soap boiler, Daniel Webster was the son of a poor farmer; Christopher Columbus was the son of a weaver; and so I could continue! So, today, realize that God can use you against all the odds. Your family background does not need to limit you. So often we feel that if we were not brought up in a Christian home then we are at a disadvantage if we want to do something outstanding for God. I believe that it is often the recent convert who has the courage to stand for Christ. So run against the odds and know that God will help you.

Florence Nightingale (1820–1910) was a celebrated English nurse, writer, and statistician. Florence, a Christian, really believed that God had called her to be a nurse, much to her family's horror. She pioneered her new nursing practices during the Crimean War, introducing night rounds when she would further examine the wounded soldiers. This was a totally new concept of care. After this she became well known and was affectionately called "The Lady with the Lamp". Nightingale laid the foundation of professional nursing with the establishment, in 1860, of her nursing school at St Thomas' Hospital in London. This was the first nursing school in the world, and is now part of King's College London. Inspired by an encounter with God in February 1837 while at her family home, Embley Park, Florence obeyed His call and announced her decision to enter nursing in 1844, despite the intense anger and distress of her mother and sister. In doing this, she rebelled against the expected role for a woman of her wealthy status, which was to become a wife and mother. Nightingale worked hard to educate herself in the art and science of nursing, in spite of opposition from her family and the restrictive societal code for affluent young English women. Nightingale was courted by politician and poet Richard Monckton Milnes, 1st Baron Houghton, but finally refused his proposal as she was convinced that this marriage would interfere with her ability to follow the call of God to nurse. Against all the opposition of her wealthy family, she obeyed her call, fulfilled her task, and transformed the nursing profession. Now the baton is passed to us. Will we be those people who will stand, even in times of adversity, and sacrifice wealth, reputation, and position to fulfil the call of God upon our lives? Sometimes the cost is high but the reward is greater. Will you run this race?

HEARTCRY OF PRAYER:

Jesus, I pray that You would help me overcome every battle in my mind and every obstacle in my life, and enable me to fulfil my call. Give me the courage, such as that shown by Florence Nightingale, to fulfil my call even when family or others do not understand my faith. Help me to win, never giving up, even against the odds. Amen.

... something worth dying for!

DAY 39 GOOD, BETTER, OR BEST?

ACTIVATION AND FOCUS:

As we strive to win, we must remember that it is not only the fact that we finish that is important, but also how we finish. To truly finish as a champion we must complete our race with our integrity and character intact. There are many champions in the world whose public success is outstanding, but whose private life is a shambles. We are called not only to make a significant impact publicly, but also to leave a legacy of peace in our homes. The best medal we can ever win is the respect and honour of our children.

> **Proverbs 3:3–4**
>
> Let love and faithfulness never leave you; bind them around your neck, write them on the tablet of your heart. Then you will win favour and a good name in the sight of God and man.
>
> **Galatians 1:10**
>
> Am I now trying to win the approval of men, or of God? Or am I trying to please men? If I were still trying to please men, I would not be a servant of Christ.

When my husband, Gordon, was leaving his recent job, the church presented him with a book of thanks, but the page that touched me most was the inscription written by our son. Here he honoured his dad for his character and leadership, in our home and in public. These "medals" are worth more than gold. In our eagerness to achieve we can often steamroller over other people's dreams, and not recognize their gifting in our quest to find our own. This competitiveness that can

easily enter our race damages so many precious people. Ask God for the medal of favour to touch your life. Win the hearts of those you work with, and help them run their race even at the expense of your own. I am so grateful to Gordon for the many times he has sacrificed, taken care of the children when they were young, and looked after the home to release me to run my race. These books could never have been written unless I was married to someone who respected my race too. So look around you and consider those people you should help inspire and accelerate in life.

But more than living a life of integrity, we must be inspired by the right motivation. Most of us have to battle the need for the approval of man at some time in our lives. Maybe you are still waiting for your dad to finally acknowledge you have made significant achievements, or you want your pastor to value your gifting and contribution to the church. Perhaps you struggle with constant thoughts of what certain friends would feel if they discovered your passion. Whatever the approval you are seeking, it will be a massive distraction in your race if you do not deal with it! So you need to fix your eyes on the right picture, the face of Jesus at the finishing line, and run for Him. I used to be intimidated by a scowl of disapproval from a member of the congregation when I was preaching. Often it would distract me and I would try to win his approval as I spoke, but I have learned rather to watch the face of Jesus and let Him reward me! After all, I will never have everyone as my friend but I must have Jesus. Now let us consider another man of courage who ran his race of sacrifice with this motivation of pleasing Jesus.

Samuel Zwemer (1867–1952) is famous for his missionary work among Muslims, and his life challenges us to endure sacrifice. In July 1904 he lost both his daughters in the Middle East when they died within eight days of each other due to the hardship and extreme heat. Nevertheless, when Zwemer reflected on this season fifty years later he was able to write, "The sheer joy of it all comes back. Gladly would I do it all over again." For many of us this sentiment is offensive, but Zwemer could now see the harvest from this costly sacrifice. As a result of his direct pioneering work, four mission stations were established, and though only small in number, "the converts showed unusual courage in professing their faith." St Christopher's Cathedral in Bahrain, birthed by this sacrifice, still continues to this day. It is impossible to know how many people were touched by the large numbers of tracts and Scripture that Zwemer distributed. However, through his work with the Student Volunteer Movement 14,000 young people have been inspired and gone out onto the mission field.

It is not easy to understand death and sacrifice, especially of loved ones. Often these circumstances can bring disapproval from family and friends, but we need to hear God and obey. We know that Hannah was challenged to give Samuel to God, so she took him to the Temple where he remained with the prophet Eli and never returned home. However, when Abraham was instructed to sacrifice Isaac on Mount Moriah God provided a ram in the thicket, so Abraham was able to lift his son off the altar and bring

him home. These are mysteries, but we must not get offended in times of sacrifice. Instead we should yield to God's will, and keep our character sweet and our motivation right, whatever the challenges we face.

HEARTCRY OF PRAYER:

So, Father, help me to finish well, looking like a champion. Let honour and integrity surround my life. Help me be someone who inspires others to find their calling too. Help me notice other gifted people and facilitate them with my resources and abilities. Father, I thank You for all grace upon my life. Let me bring You joy! Amen.

DAY 40

MORE THAN GOLD

ACTIVATION AND FOCUS:

Pat Riley states, "A champion needs a motivation above and beyond winning." I pray that this motivation will be the joy on the face of Jesus when you finish your race. As a child I often used to daydream about going to heaven and wondered what God would say to me. I always wanted to see His face full of joy, and imagined Him picking me up and squeezing me with the biggest hug, and then saying, "Rachel, you lived your life well!" This reward would be worth more than gold! I do not know what you picture in your mind, but let our prize at the end of the race be to bring Him great pleasure.

> **Philippians 3:13–15**
>
> Brothers, I do not consider myself yet to have taken hold of it. But one thing I do: Forgetting what is behind and straining towards what is ahead, I press on towards the goal to win the prize for which God has called me heavenwards in Christ Jesus. All of us who are mature should take such a view of things.

A brave man, C. T. Studd, was known for his mistakes and poor people skills but passionate vision. C. T. Studd (1860–1931) was an English missionary who faithfully served God in China, India, and Africa. His motto was: "If Jesus Christ is God and died for me, then no sacrifice can be too great for me to make for Him." Studd

Something to live for...

is remembered as both a cricketer and a missionary. As a cricketer he played for England in the 1882 match won by Australia which was the origins of the Ashes. As a missionary to China he was part of the group known as "the Cambridge Seven", and was later responsible for setting up the Heart of Africa Mission, which became the Worldwide Evangelisation Crusade (now WEC International). This man touched nations, lived by faith, and, with his wife, Priscilla, trusted God for thousands of pounds. He was ostracized by many of his wealthy friends, but he left a legacy greater than money in three nations.

I was twenty-four years old when I nearly died as the result of a road traffic accident in Zimbabwe. These near death encounters have an incredible way of focusing our priorities. I decided then that I would not let fear get in the way of my dreams. I needed to live my life well, even if it was different from the expected norm, and fulfil the calling on my life. On my race I have been criticized for doing what I do because some have felt that such a leadership role is not appropriate for a woman. But I cannot change my call or my gender! I have been misunderstood and accused of being too passionate when I have spoken strongly of the needs in our nation. However, this has not been the sound of female emotion but the cry of a passionate heart seeking to serve God. I have felt intimidated, overwhelmed, and totally incapable, but one thing I know – I must run my race. I do not have the greatest degree or training, the largest financial backing, or the most impressive arguments. But one thing I know: I have been called to love people and touch nations with the power of God. So what burns inside of you? Do not let others quench your fire. Run your race and WIN!

As I was praying for the UK recently I felt God give me this promise. He spoke to me from the Christmas tree lights that I had just removed from my tree. Each light was very small, they were micro fairy lights, but when wound together around my Christmas tree they had been very bright. So God said to me, "The revival and awakening that you seek to see in your nation will not happen in a moment of incredible breakthrough, but will come as the result of an army of dedicated people who have consistently done the right thing in their neighbourhoods." He further spoke and said, "It will be the steady, obedient work of thousands that will reverse the curse of the enemy in this nation! Each one must play their part as, if one light goes out, a whole area will be without light. Tell the people that every life counts. Each one must take their place!" So it is time for you to respond, turn your light on, and **run the race of your life!**

HEARTCRY OF PRAYER:

Father, I want to run this race and bring You pleasure. Let me be part of the army that transforms my nation. Remove from my life everything that would hinder this call. Raise up in the nations an army of warriors who will fearlessly carry Your name. Amen.

RUN THE RACE
OF YOUR LIFE!

Something to live for... something worth dying for!

DEDICATED HEROES

DETERMINED COURAGE

DEVOTED TO PURITY

DISCIPLINED SACRIFICE

DANGEROUS PASSION

DESTINED AS CHAMPIONS

ABOUT THE AUTHOR

Rachel Hickson is an internationally respected prayer leader and Bible teacher with a recognized prophetic gift. She teaches all over the world, and is in demand as a conference speaker.

At the age of twenty-four Rachel, with her husband, Gordon, was working alongside Reinhard Bonnke and the Christ for All Nations team in Africa. After just six weeks in Zimbabwe she almost lost her life in a horrific car accident, but was miraculously healed by God. This incident birthed in Rachel a desire to pray and to train others to realize the full potential of a praying church.

After returning from Africa in 1990, Rachel and Gordon pastored a group of four churches in Hertfordshire and it was during this time that they established Heartcry Ministries with the call to train and equip people to be released into effective ministries. In 2005 Rachel and Gordon moved to Oxford where Gordon was the associate minister of St Aldates Church for six years. In 2011 he moved to become the director of specialist missions and church planting projects, still based in Oxford.

Rachel travels internationally, visiting Europe, North America, Africa, India and Australia. Invitations come from a variety of denominational backgrounds, and both rural and city churches.

Rachel and Gordon have a passion to see cities transformed through the power of prayer and evangelism. One of their projects linked churches and prayer ministries across London, and developed a strategy called the London Prayernet.

Rachel has been married to Gordon for over thirty years. She is a mother of two married children, Nicola and David, and has two grandchildren, Leila and Cooper.

She is the author of eight books:
Supernatural Communication: the Privilege of Prayer
Supernatural Breakthrough: the Heartcry for Change
(published by New Wine Ministries)

Stepping Stones to Freedom
Pathway of Peace
Eat the Word, Speak the Word
Run Your Race
(published by Monarch Books)

Eat the Word Study Guide
Supernatural Communication Study Guide
(published by Heartcry for Change)

HEARTCRY MINISTRIES AND HEARTCRY FOR CHANGE

We work with churches and people from many nations and denominations to equip them in the following areas:

- **PRAYER** – Training an army of ordinary people in prayer schools and seminars to become confident to break the sound barrier and pray informed, intelligent and passionate prayers.

- **PROPHETIC** – Equipping the church to be an accurate prophetic voice in the nation by teaching in training schools and conferences the principles of the prophetic gift. We seek to train people who are passionate to know the presence of God, are available to hear His voice and then learn to speak His word with accuracy so that lives can be touched and changed.

- **WOMEN** – Delivering a message of hope to women across the nations and cultures to help them arise with a new confidence so that they can be equipped and ready to fulfil their destiny and execute their kingdom purpose.

- **CAPITAL CITIES** – Standing in the capital cities of the world, working with government institutions, businesses and the church and then crying out for a new alignment of the natural and spiritual government in these places. A cry for London and beyond.

- **BUSINESS & FINANCE** – Connecting business people with their kingdom purpose so that provision can partner more effectively with vision and accelerate the purpose of God in nations. Connecting commerce, community and church for change!

- **LEADERS OF TOMORROW** – Mentoring and encouraging younger leaders to pioneer the next move of God in the areas of politics and government, social action and justice issues, creative arts, media and the ministry.

- **NATIONS** – Partnering with nations in Africa, the Middle East and India by supplying teaching, training and practical resources to strengthen and resource them as they work for breakthrough in their nations.

- **MEDIA, TV & SATELLITE** – Developing training materials to equip and disciple the church in the nations to understand and fulfil their responsibility. To be a voice of encouragement through TV into the homes of the army of ordinary people praying for impossible situations.

- **RESOURCES & CONFERENCES** – Writing books, manuals and training materials that will equip the church to be prepared. Running conferences and training days where leaders and the church can be encouraged to continue in their purpose and calling.

Heartcry hopes to continue strengthening the Church to connect with their community whilst encouraging the people to hear the urgent call to prayer. Now is the time to pray and cry out for our land and continent and watch what God will do for us!

Heartcry Ministries
P.O. Box 737
Oxford, Oxon
OX1 9FA
UK

Heartcry for Change USA
P.O. Box 2354
Kirkland
WA 98083
USA

www.heartcry.co.uk
www.heartcry.us
www.heartcryforchange.com

PICTURE ACKNOWLEDGMENTS

iStockphoto: p. 6 Maridav; p. 12 Sacha Bloor

Corbis: p. 91; p. 15 John Henley; p. 19 Mike Kemp/Rubberball; p. 21 Lava/beyond; p. 25 Rolf Kosecki; p. 28 Uli Wiesmeier; p. 30 Simon Jarratt; p. 34 Roy McMahon; p. 36 Michel Setboun; p. 39 Larry Williams; pp. 41, 72 Ben Welsh; p. 43 Richard Hamilton Smith; p. 45 Nice One Productions; p. 46 Edith Held; p. 49 Imagemore Co., Ltd.; p. 50 Doug Berry/Blend Images; pp. 54, 147 Image Source; p. 59 David Pickford/Robert Harding World Imagery; p. 60 Daniel H. Bailey; p. 63 Ron Nickel/Design Pics; p. 66 John Rensten/cultura; p. 69 Artiga Photo; p. 77 Peter Beck; pp. 81, 94, 161 Pete Saloutos/Blend Images; p. 84 Nick Dolding/cultura; p. 87 Darren Kemper; p. 88 Blasius Erlinger; p. 97 Zac Macaulay/cultura; p. 99 Hill Street Studios/Blend Images; pp. 100, 120 Randy Faris; p. 106 Erik Isakson/Tetra Images; p. 110 Jen Rosenstein; p. 113 Ingolf Hatz; pp. 117, 155 John Norris; p. 123 Ocean; p. 125 Jon Hicks; p. 127 Images.com; p. 133 KidStock/Blend Images; p. 134 Tom Grill; p. 137 Robert Michael; p. 144 Matt Gibson/LOOP IMAGES/Loop Images; p. 150 Bettmann

Getty: pp. 75, 139, 141, 153, 159, 163; p. 11 Javier Pierini; pp. 17, 22 AFP; p. 53 Karl Weatherly; p. 57 Alistair Berg; p. 79 Nick Daly; p. 102 Tetra Images; p. 118 Jim Cummins; p. 129 Anders Blomqvist; p. 166 Darren Robb; p. 170 John Kelly

Alamy: p. 33 Dunca Daniel Mihai